New Hampshire Tales

New Hampshire Tales

Henry Caryl Hallas

RivuletFerryPress.com

Published by the Rivulet Ferry Press, Farmingdale, New York

© 2017 Henry Caryl Hallas

Printed in the United States of America

For information, contact the Rivulet Ferry Press, Farmingdale, New York, www.RivuletFerryPress.com

ISBN: 978-0-9977233-4-2

10 9 8 7 6 5 4 3 2 1

To

Mary Louisa Caryl Hallas

and

Benjamin Henry Stahl, Teddy Dunn Stahl, Hayden

Anders Riddle, and Tallaby Katherine Riddle

Table of Contents

Acknowledgments

I have dedicated *New Hampshire Tales* to my mother, Mary Louisa Caryl Hallas. She was a very good writer in her own right and always encouraged me to write. Her sensitive reflections on "place" are reflected in this piece.

Additionally, I have dedicated this collection to my grandchildren: Benjamin Henry Stahl, Teddy Dunn Stahl, Hayden Anders Riddle, and Tallaby Katherine Riddle. My hope is that some day they will read this and reflect on the various inspirations, observations, and insights contained herein. I was deeply imprinted by my childhood experiences at the farm in New Hampshire.

My writing about this "Place" began 24 years ago in 1993. That was a fertile period of discovery regarding the history and legends pre-dating the Hallas presence on what is now called "Blueberry Meadow Farm." My current writing on this "Place" is usually inspired by nature happenings of the moment, and they therefore tend to be "when the spirit moves" pieces. Many of the *New Hampshire Cabin Tales* were originally emails to various family members and friends who periodically would encourage me to assemble and publish them. So, I also wish to acknowledge the generous encouragement of our friends, Nancy, Gerry, and Jennifer, along with my daughters, Kate and Liz, who also shared their encouragement.

A special acknowledgement goes to my editor, proofreader and wonderful wife Louise, who has also been my sidekick during many of the Tales. She has helped me overcome (somewhat) my fear of English teachers. So, it remains a "work in progress." However, enough water has flowed over the dam that I was inspired to put my thoughts on paper and assemble the disparate pieces.

Introduction

This writing is backwards looking. It explains some of the history of my relationship with a special farm in rural New Hampshire. Much, but not all, deals with the history of our farm from my parents' acquisition and before. I guess I would say the majority of it deals with what one would call "place."

This book begins with a simple letter written by my mother. Her letter describes how the farm came into the family. She wanted to leave this note for her grandchildren. I follow that piece with an amusing piece about my role in the actual family decision at age 5. The book then branches out to a somewhat disconnected series of historical sketches and tales, hence the title *New Hampshire Tales*.

One section contains some personal sketches of people I have met on this journey. The final section becomes more personal and current with "Cabin Tales" which were written primarily to capture the essence of nature events at a log cabin I built near the farm.

.

1

* * *

"This Old Farm"
1940's to Present

THIS OLD FARM
BY MARY LOUISA HALLAS

Come out on the porch and sit in the old rocking chairs and Gramma will tell you some stories. Would you like to hear how your Grandmother and Grandfather found this old farm?

Well a long time ago when your Daddies were a little bigger than you are (1946: Hank 5, Herb 8), Grandfather and I decided to find a quiet little place in the country. Life had become hectic with a newspaper and other jobs. We spent many Sundays driving all around different little towns in Connecticut but couldn't find what we wanted. Then we ventured to the nearby state of New Hampshire. And right here in these lovely hills we knew this is where we wanted to be. Grandfather called it "God's country where the soft Pine trees grow."

Grandma liked it too for several reasons. First, before I-91 was built, your Daddies liked to ride in the car just so long, then they would get to punching and fooling around the way boys do. And just about this far was all Gramma could take – she tired of saying, "sit down and be good boys." Secondly, as much as Grandpa liked the woods, Grandma liked the clear lakes to go swim in. Here the lake water is so clear you can see the bottom and our own brook runs over the rocks and through the meadows. A lady that used to live here and cook for the lumbermen (Emily Whitney) said that I

could drink the brook water – they used to as the water starts way back in the hills with springs and Grandma's house is the first house near it.

Some friends of Grandpa told us this old farm might be bought but several people had tried. The trouble was Mr. Perry owned it and had grown up here as a boy.... in fact it had been in his family for years. We went to see him and your Grandpa was a very persuasive man. He was tall, handsome and had very deep blue eyes under heavy dark eyebrows. But he was direct, forward and honest and when he told Mr. Perry he would like to buy his family home because we want to come to the Farm from the crowded city and our busy life and also where two boys could enjoy nature in the woods and fields.

Mr. Perry listened and said only "Yep" and "Nope" and picked up his milking pail and turned to the cow shed and said, "I'll let you know."

Two weeks went by and Grandpa and I decided we would have to start looking again. When in the mail came a 1-cent postcard saying only
"You can have the place – yours truly
A. Perry".

FIRST ONE IN!

The previous pages contain a lovely portrait written by my mom so that her grandchildren would understand something about how "The Farm" came into the family's possession. Here is my recollection as a 5-year-old. And now "the rest of the story" as Paul Harvey was famous for saying.

A few years ago, I was ruminating about all the changes Louise and I have brought to the farm. And then a light bulb went off in my head.....I had been the very first one of the family to set foot inside the farm! Here's the story.

My parents had been driving around southern New Hampshire looking for a place for many months. I recall we looked at a house (formerly called The Opera Singer's house). It was and still is a very lovely spot; however, my Mom was spooked by garter snakes on the back patio and nixed that choice. We also had looked at another house nearby (currently a horse farm). That also was quite lovely; however, it was really way too big for our needs. Many houses in the area were available, since the economic effects of the Great Depression and World War II were very much a reality in New England. Many of the really old houses of the "first settlers" (of this country) had been abandoned during the Depression or had fallen in on themselves to become stone foundation cellar holes.

A family friend from Connecticut, who owned a neat old farmhouse on the same road, had mentioned that "The Perry Place" might be for sale. The family piled into the car, a deep maroon 1940 Coupe, and headed to the house from Bill's farm. A couple miles to the south, we crossed the brook and started up the hill towards "The Perry Place". My mother was somewhat horrified since the dirt road was more like an old logging road with ruts and stones and no passing lane with a deep ravine dropping to a gorgeous brook.

We drove about another mile up the hill until it leveled out and came to a very decrepit abandoned farm which my Dad declared was "The Perry Place". We pulled into the farmyard. To our far right I could see a half filled corncrib. Next, to the left were a large and very weathered carriage shed and a carriage sitting in front of it. Next, to the left was the beginning of the "L" of the farmhouse and then the main farmhouse with a wrap-around porch. The whole place looked pretty shot from the outside. The windows were either broken or so weathered that the panes might fall out with the next gust. The shingles were ajar on the roof with several holes evident. The clapboards gave a mere suggestion that the farmhouse might have been painted white with a dark blue trim. Many clapboards were hanging by a thread and a spare nail or two. It was a pretty sad picture. Around back there was a one and a half story first settler's cabin that had at some point been repurposed into use as a "Sugarhouse" (a place where maple sap was boiled down into maple syrup). It also looked like the next gust might topple it. To the left of the "Sugar house" there was a series of chicken coops and finally an ox cart shed deeper up "Old Bryant Road". Behind us across the dirt road were the still-standing remains of a once proud 3 story red barn, which then looked more grey and was only a half story, which was rotting as we looked. All in all it was pretty forlorn, and evidence of neglect was everywhere. The grass in the farmyard matched the wild hay in the ancient apple orchard up the hillside to the north.

My parents were smitten by the charm of the location. My mother had already fallen in love with the wrap-around porch and my Dad was expounding on the beauty of the trout brook nearby on the property. I suspect they were trying to comment on the positives, since Herb and I probably gave away our dismay by the looks on our faces. Our parents had vision of what might be, whereas Herb and I could only see exactly what was in front of us.

We all walked up to the house and peeked in the windows. My mother really wanted to get a better sense of what lay inside. To them the house was like a Christmas present whose wrapping teased you to guess what charm lay inside. Both parents tried to open the front door, no luck. They then tried to open the front windows, also with no luck. We all circled the house checking window after window.

On the backside of the farmhouse (which faced both the Orchard and the Sugarhouse) we came to a partially broken window. The lower half had some panes missing, and the wood, which would hold them, was cracked severely. My brother promptly said he could likely fit through and wanted Dad's approval to do so. No luck, as his frame was just too big to slide through the opening. All eyes then turned to me as if they were sizing up a turkey for a small oven. I immediately knew what they were thinking and I wanted no part of it. I was already spooked by the outside of the house and didn't even want to imagine what the inside might hold.....maybe Herb was brave, but I was the family coward on this deal! I quickly learned that a 5-year-old doesn't have much standing to object to what the family desired. This position was oft repeated during my formative years. I wasn't old enough to drink; I wasn't old enough to vote and I wasn't old enough to tell my parents "no way am I going inside this creepy old farm house!"

It was all "take one for the team!"

Before I knew it my Dad had me up in the air by my belt and breeches and my brother was pushing my head and shoulders through the opening while my mom was telling me what was expected for the soon-to-be-completed home inspection by her 5-year-old. I was the live drone with a built-in computer to record and report all upon retrieval. I was so worried about getting cut by the broken glass of the window I never fully paid much attention to Mom's plea for information. I fell to the floor inside onto a pile of trash and debris.

I stood up and looked back out the window from whence I had come hoping I would get a governor's pardon. Not to be, as all three chimed in with instructions to search the house and report back to HQ. I slowly turned around and surveyed the room and beyond. Luckily, nothing seemed to move; however, all the rooms were littered with glass, old newspapers, and old farmhouse stuff. I slowly began to wander from room to room. My thinking was that the faster I looked now; maybe the faster I could get the hell out. I suspected I would be bombed by bats, spiders and maybe even a skunk inside the house. Having never made a home inspection, I was totally clueless about what to look for or report back on. I was totally taken by the mess inside....the old newspapers, the cans, the broken chairs and on and on....the stuff my parents didn't care about. I totally whiffed on how many rooms, the size of the rooms, where the windows and doors were.....you name it and I remained clueless.

I stumbled into the kitchen and then out to the "L" and did notice some old black iron cooking pots; they were kind of cool to me. I took one look at the room of the "L" and thought I heard a mouse, so I bolted back to the back room where I had entered the house to jump back out of the window to the waiting arms of my parents.

The debriefing session did not go well.

How many rooms?.................I don't know.

What was the size of the Kitchen?.................I don't know.

What were the colors of the wallpaper? ....What's wallpaper?

Where was the bathroom?.........I didn't see one Mom, really. (I was right on this one since the bathroom was a privy behind the house near the carriage barn!)

What kind of floors were there?.....I couldn't see the floor because of the trash, honest!

Was there running water or did it have a pump?............What's a pump?

Net-net, my sortie was next to useless and all three of them seemed to agree on that point. I really hated this place. I did hold out hope for some fun with the trout brook however.

Real Horseshoes

Our first sets of horseshoes were made of rubber. The year was 1946 and rubber products were beginning to reappear in the marketplace after World War II. I suspect they were a Christmas gift from Dad to my brother and me to keep us occupied in the basement of our Connecticut home. They came with two rubber plates, which held wooden pins as targets. There were four brown rubber horseshoes about the size of a grown lady's hand and four round hoops made from rope. You had two games: ring toss or mighty rubber horseshoes. Herb and I spent many hours in the basement, first throwing the hoops or shoes at the wooden stake and eventually (if either was losing) we would start to throw them at each other. Suffice it to say rubber and rope usually didn't hurt anyone, but the younger brother was known to whine a lot about it.

When the family acquired the farm in New Hampshire, it quickly became a source of great exploration and discovery. There was the brook, the "big rocks," the carriage shed, the ox shed, and the meadow. Every weekend held some new adventure and some new discovery. One such discovery happened in what we now call the "Magic Shed." This was a shed attached to the "L" of the house that housed the oxen originally. It had a dirt floor and tons of old horse straps, metal pails, nails,

11

spikes, pitchforks, and such. My dad decided to add some metal shelving in the shed to house his personal nail collection....there wasn't a hardware store where Dad didn't walk out a few pounds heavier with a bag of 10-penny nails or such. While attempting to level the metal shelving, he hit a metal pile near one of the corners and had to pull it all out in order to get the shelf level. The pile happened to be 10 or so real old horseshoes, hand forged, and none of them matched. This was a spectacular find for my Mom and Dad; you'd think they were pure gold. However, to me and my brother they looked somewhat similar to the rubber horseshoes we had in our basement in Connecticut. My brother Herb picked one up and began tossing it in the front farmyard, much to the dismay of my mother. His accuracy was suspect and the family car shared the front yard. Mom called to Dad in her very sweet voice and said something about how the boys might need to relocate the throwing area if horseshoes were to become a New Hampshire game. My Dad agreed and scratched his head while thinking about where to send his little "chuckers." Meanwhile I began rummaging through the shoes to find the biggest, as anyone knows the biggest is always the best. I found one full-sized and one half-size. My brother claimed the second biggest and another somewhat half-size. The shoes were really cool and still had horseshoe nails in them!

Dad decided we could play in a spot parallel to the front stone wall at the beginning of the meadow to the north of the house. That decision in 1947 still holds today, and that area is still known as the "Pits." They have never moved in 70 years of brotherly competition! Dad located a few mismatched metal pins in the "Magic Shed" and hammered them into the ground. Let the games begin! I quickly realized that I could only heave the large shoe halfway to the opposite pin, and Herb could sail them all the way. So, the first swap took place. I sought the smallest shoes and Herb claimed the biggest....foxed again!

Over that summer we played and played and played.....and I got beaten, beaten, beaten....something I was already accustomed to because of my brother's athletic skills. My hands would occasionally get cuts from the old nails and Mom was concerned about lockjaw and such, so she convinced Dad to get some "unreal" Picnic Horseshoes by the end of the summer. The Real Horseshoes were returned to the "Magic Shed" to await another archeological discovery in some future day.

As I grew older and stronger, I became a better opponent; however, Herb always kicked it up a notch and became a better and better chucker. Still, we were only the local champs of the farm and Herb had only beaten me. He decided to stretch his wings and see if he could beat another "chucker" down the hill, My Dad's friend, Bill. Bill's horseshoe reputation was known far and wide. We frequently would see him pitching away along his front stone fence near his farmhouse. You could always tell when Bill was throwing, because you'd hear the sound of metal on metal, a sure sign of a good thrower.

13

CHAPTER 1

Eventually Herb got his nerve up and mentioned that perhaps he could have a match with Bill. I forget the actual results. I know Herb acquitted himself well but Bill was too good and Bill remained undefeated. That match did one thing, however, and that was to solidify the type of rotation that my brother began using....it was a one and a half spin that would rotate in the air and then open up to smack the pin and hold to the pin for a ringer. My throwing style was an end-over-end that would fork the pin and or reject back off....forever to be called a "REJECT."

Over the years, Herb and I have played hundreds and hundreds of games. He has won roughly 90% of them. My only game of fame was our last game in October 2000. After I won, I refused any rematch, as I wanted to end the millennium as the winner of the year of Y2K.

In my late 40s, I began to pitch a fair amount of horseshoes. I could beat my friends regularly and I could even beat Herb fairly often....but how good was I? I decided to venture off the mountain and go to the big city and find out. Now when it comes to big cities and horseshoes none are bigger than a nearby town in New Hampshire! It has hosted numerous county and state championships and even a world championship in the 1970s! Its stadium was located in a local park which has a concession stand building, lights for night throwing, a flag and a large scoreboards as well as bleachers. The throwing area consists of 10 lanes made of concrete with clay pits and wooden backboards. It's a primo site. I had watched matches there a few times, but never had the nerve to actually bring my shoes to town.

I decided a Monday night would be best, since all the very serious throwers would be gone after Friday, Saturday, or Sunday. It turned out that appeared to be a good move, as only 4 of 10 pits were being contested. That meant I could practice alone on the fifth lane. I had never thrown into a clay pit, so that was exciting! It was, however, a good news/ bad news deal. The good news was that the clay would stop the shoe dead and you wouldn't have the shoe slide or roll out of sight. The bad news was that if you missed the 3'x3' clay pit, the shoe would hit the concrete walkway, and you'd hear a clang that would echo all around the pine trees. Heads would turn to see who the new rookie was!

I practiced about 45 minutes and noticed that only one other lane had two men throwing. I watched awhile and they seemed to be pretty good. Eventually the younger man said he had to leave. The older man began to pick up his shoes. He had dark green coveralls on and looked like he had worked all day at a local gas station....how good could he be dressed like that, I thought. So, I mustered my courage and asked if he'd like to pitch a round or two. He turned and said "sure" in a deep New Hampshire accent. He looked about 70 and had wrinkles from ear to ear and dark brown suntanned leather skin. We warmed up a few times up and back and then we began. Good horseshoe players, I have since learned, are ranked by their ringer percentage. In a typical competition in big city tournaments, you'll

15

usually see that someone who throws between 30 to 50% ringers will typically win. Lesser brackets will throw a lower percentage. The typical tournament in that park would have flights of A to D-level throwers. I believe you must have a 40% ringer average to qualify for the A level bracket. I didn't have a clue what my percentage was, but guessing now in hindsight, I would probably be between 20% and 40% on my very best days ever. Herb was close to 50% on his best days. Well, to make a long story short, my dark green coverall opponent shot 90+% for 4 games in a row. I shot 30 to 35%....which was great for me, but needless to say, I was humbled. He was very kind and friendly and said he'd be happy to continue since he had nowhere to go. I couldn't wait until the slaughter was over and I could return to being the near champion of Our Hill. When we finished, I noticed he had a special battered wooden case to hold his shoes. When he closed the case, I saw "New Hampshire State Champion" for about 6 different years......oh my, had I misread my opponent. I've never returned to "big city" horseshoes.

THE KEG OF NAILS

It was the summer of 1953 and this 12-year-old boy was quite excited about taking a solo trout-fishing excursion down the Brook. The first step in such an adventure was to dig the worms. There were only two spots on the farm that held good trout worms. The first was behind the house near the privy. The land sloped away and was always moist and dark with leaf decay. The only hazard was that occasionally you might come across broken bottles, which could cut your fingers when you searched the soil for the worms. The second site was across the road where the cows would feed on the east side of the rotting barn. There was a depression there that was always moist and held decaying leaves. I never could be sure which of these two spots held the day's worm catch, but one or the other always did!

I placed about 15 small trout-sized worms into a green metal worm container that you wore on your belt. I think the container was called "Old Pal." I then gathered up the rest of my gear: my trout creel over one shoulder and my Dad's trusty fishing rod and a straw hat to help repel the bugs. I yelled to my Mom that I was headed to fish the Brook down to the old mill site. She came to the screen door and asked me to pick up a red wooden sap bucket if I saw one in the woods. The old steam mill at the bottom of the hill had burned down in the late 1890's

17

and an inventory of red wooden sap buckets was stacked in the woods against the old stone foundation. New Hampshire white pine is quite durable apparently.

I wandered down the dirt road to the section of the brook that is north of the farm. It was a delightful day of fishing this beautiful section of the brook, which has a cascade of small trout pools running about a mile down hill. I had caught about 5 or 6 trout, all slightly over 6 inches, just perfect for breakfast. I worked my way downhill to the base of the hill close to another old farmhouse. Much to my surprise, curiosity, and attention, there was an auction in progress at the farmhouse. You can't imagine how exciting this was to a boy of 12 with his fishing pole, worms and boots. An auction was an adult thing, something Mom and Dad occasionally went to and spent some precious dollars for items which ended up as prized possessions. There I was....with no parents at an adult event! How cool is that?!

I recall it took a bit of courage to ease up to the farmyard scene, at first to observe and then to become engaged. I watched many items come and go.....at some point I reached into my pocket to see if I had any money.....surely Mom and Dad would want me to snare a bargain, some great antique.....consider the possibilities! The fishing expedition had become a discovery, an opportunity, a chance to land a big one. "Get real," my inner voice said....big deal! 6 cents was all I could find in my pocket. Oh well, nothing ventured nothing gained. It took awhile, but I decided to jump into the action with my 6 cents. Eventually I sidled up to the front and whispered "6 cents" at any item that caught my eye. The Auctioneer would ignore me and continue to sell item after item. Obviously, I had to change my strategy. I had to get more aggressive! So, I raised my voice and bid on almost every item. Again, the Auctioneer ignored my 6-cent bids. The people nearby snickered. But I had my pride at stake. I had to win something; something I could bring home to show Mom and Dad. I had come this far....I had to hang in there.

I suspect in retrospect the Auctioneer eventually found me to be the pest I had become. Being a veteran, his strategy to deal with me was quick and simple. He looked around his table for anything he knew would not sell easily and was more trouble than it was worth to those attending. He spied a half keg of nails in a small old wooden barrel (too heavy for most to carry away) and a dingy old kerosene lantern (not yet a sought-after item due to the recent arrival of electricity in the area in 1952). He put the two items up on the table and said, "Now what do I have for these two items"........"Six Cents!" I said. "Sold" said the Auctioneer. The two hard-to-sell items and the pest were gone! Next item please.

I took my prizes to the bushes by the brook and hid them there with my trout and my Dad's pole. There was no way that I could carry all these things back up the hill to the farm, so my parents would have to drive back down to pick up the nails and my gear. I then walked up the hill swinging the lantern to show off to my parents. My Mom was delighted with the lantern and Dad was thrilled with the half keg of nails to add to his treasure trove in the "Magic Shed".

Now click forward 43 years to 1995. Louise and I had been invited to dinner at the very same farm, owned then by the daughter of the 1952 owner and her husband. Both of them had been at the same auction 41 years prior, unbeknownst to me. In fact, the husband had taken some photos of the auction (which he hasn't yet located) which might....might contain yours truly. The dinner date was on January 14, 1995. As the date approached, I tried to come up with an idea to commemorate the occasion, since I had never been inside the neighboring farmhouse in my life. It seemed fitting that I should return some of the nails to their original location, assuming I could find them. In my mind's eye, I had put that half keg of nails in the Magic Shed....somewhere in a back corner. I did have great pride in this keg as a 12-year-old, because my Dad liked nails and had them in small bags everywhere.

So on a Saturday morning I went into the Magic Shed and searched for them. Bingo! It was there under a shelf in the rear of the main shed. I removed about 5 lbs. of them. Louise had a red-checkered cloth to fold them into a baggie and then I dropped them into an old "Lane Bucket" that we had picked up recently at a Local Auction. It all seemed like a neat idea.

When we arrived at the dinner, we proffered our friendship gift to Priscilla. She bent over the gift and opened it; and although I didn't notice it at first, she lost her composure, knelt down, and then teared up.

Apparently, she immediately recognized the nails. The keg of nails was a favorite plaything for her as a girl. Whenever she needed to nail something or build a small project, she said she would go to that keg for the nails which were in the garage near the back door. This was an amazing memory moment for all of us. Additionally, it turned out that the bucket was a "Lane Bucket" and Mr. Lane was a friend of her family. Pricilla's father and Mr. Lane were both selectmen together when she was a child. Priscilla was as excited about the bucket as the nails. You have to love living history!

POST-WORLD WAR II

World War II had a tremendous impact on our small-town world. We had three uncles in the South Pacific theater, beginning with Uncle Terry who was at Pearl Harbor on Ford's Island when his PBY squadron got blown up, Uncle Bohdan who was a Captain of a U.S. Army company that spent time at Iwo Jima, and finally, Uncle Henry, a fighting "Seabee" whose colorblindness kept him from joining the Marines. My Mom and Dad served on the home front by sending a weekly newsletter to the soldiers overseas from our Town. The newsletter became the germ of the weekly newspaper business that supported our family during my childhood through college.

A number of anecdotes, which have a post-World War II New Hampshire connection, relate to the War's impact on post-war life at the farm. Here's a string of unrelated vignettes.

The Parking Lot

One late fall Saturday in November of 1947, the family piled into the family car for a day trip to check the farm before the winter snows. The normal practice in those years was to close the farm down in late October. This particular year our day trip coincided with the beginning of the New Hampshire deer-hunting season. As we drove in on our dirt road, we began to notice a few cars and an occasional truck parked along the dirt road. Some were empty and some had hunters lounging mid-morning with rifles leaning up against the sides of the vehicles. This was most exciting to a 6-year-old.

As we pulled up to the farm, we were very surprised to see that our entire front yard and barnyard were wall to wall with vehicles; perhaps there were 15 to 20. Additionally there were seven or eight men standing or sitting on our porch, all with rifles and dressed in various types of red buffalo plaids and caps and leather boots. My parents were alarmed and thought something must have happened to the farm. Dad spotted one open slot to park the car and turned our car to fill the void. As he got the car halfway in, a man jumped off the porch with rifle in hand and waved him off and said that that spot belonged to "Fred" who was coming back with coffee from the store. Obviously, my Dad became apoplectic and told the man that this was his farm. The man in question replied that this farm was the central hunting location for much of the county, and they had been using it for years and years. Oh my.....times had changed! Upon reflection, it became clear that most of these men were soldiers who had recently been hunting Germans and Japanese. Some had military boots; ammo webbing and some wore bomber jackets made in a nearby New Hampshire town.

Welcome to Post-WWII New Hampshire.

P-51 Mustang Attack on the Hill

A most exciting event unfolded as I was beginning to take a nap (as directed by Mom) one summer day in 1948. I had just lain down when we heard the roar of a very loud airplane overhead. Airplane sounds were a big deal back then, because they were seldom heard or seen in the sky! I tore off the blanket and raced to the front porch in my skivvies. Herb was there hollering for me to hurry up or I'd miss it. We both reached the meadow and searched the sky to locate the sound and the aircraft. As we looked southward, there it was, high above the rotting old red barn, a U.S. Army Fighter plane! Just then the P-51 Mustang turned and banked into a dive right at us, it seemed. The pilot was making a bombing run on the red barn! Down he came out of the clouds, engine screaming as we had heard it in newsreels. Herb and I were both frozen in the meadow in our underwear as the fighter roared earthward. It got to just feet above the barn and then the pilot waggled his wings, did a barrel roll, and screamed just up above the top of the apples trees in the meadow. We could see the pilot big as life as he roared up the meadow. I later found out that the pilot was a local young man and a veteran of WWII who was raised on a nearby farm where we still buy our best summer corn. Quite breathtaking! Apparently, he had just arrived home from Europe and he wanted his neighbors to get his signature hello move. A few weeks later he returned flying a C-47 Cargo "Skytrain" transport and pulled the same move.
WOW!

Army/Navy Surplus

Our farm relied greatly on Army/Navy WWII surplus in the early days of our family's ownership. Most of it came from J.J. Johnson's (real) Army/Navy Surplus store in a nearby town.

Here's a partial list:

Navy Bunk Bed (wooden) – Herb and I used these for years. We still have half of one painted red.

Folding Army cot beds – for occasional guests;

Folding canvas bucket – to haul water out of the well before aluminum buckets became available again;

Navy white canvas cot – hung on the front porch where it was the scene of many Herb and Henry fights as to its use.

Army green surplus cans of DDT – used to repel bugs and pesky younger brothers.

U.S. Army boot oil preservative – Still in use to this day to protect leather boots from wet and snow.

U.S. Machetes – short and long made by Collinsville Company located in Connecticut. Both still in use to this day at the farm.

U.S. Army Ammo pouch and web belts – can't play war without them!

U.S. Navy long-handled trenching tool – still serviceable in "Magic Shed."

U.S. Marine knapsack – one for Herb and one for me; both still serviceable;

"Seabee" issued rain gear used for trout fishing on rainy days.

"SPAM" canned food used for occasional breakfast usually under protest

U.S. Canvas tarp....predates the "Blue or Green" tarps of today;

U.S. Navy Marine knife and holder from Uncle Terry....needed for any trip in the woods.

U.S. (or USSR) Army woolen Blankets made in a local Mill during the War......used on cold nights for decades.

We Called It "The Sugarhouse"

We always called it the "Sugarhouse," but that wasn't its original function. That was only one of its several roles over the many years. I believe the original structure was the remains of our first settlers' cabin. All that survives of the original cabin structure are the eastern foundation stones, the north and south doorway threshold entry stones and a slightly relocated pair of huge hearthstones, which Louise and I moved about 1 or 2 feet to the east before I rebuilt the fireplace.

I have very fond memories of the Sugarhouse. Here's my best recollection of its features from the 1940s. It was a half-story structure that was post and beam, wooden pegged style. It had no clapboards, merely plank wood nailed to hand-hewn beams. The doors (north and south entrance) had been removed; any and all windows were also removed. I believe the Perrys cut a wider doorway in the west wall so they could park their new "Abenaque" mobile saw mill under cover. The floor was dirt and the ceiling was about 6 plus feet high. I recall that once I got to be 6 feet tall, I had to duck to go in and out. The two threshold stones were barely noticeable, as soil had built up upon them. The most remarkable feature was an enormous "Bee Hive" brick fireplace and oven structure with a neat solid granite mantel and two enormous hearthstones. I could barely squeeze around the east back side. This old brick structure dominated the ground floor. It was slightly raised and had two fireplace openings facing west. There was a "bee hive" baking oven on the south side and a small warming oven on the north side. It was quite remarkable.

The existence of such a large and complex heating source tells me that the original use of the Sugarhouse was likely the original first cabin where our first settlers lived while they were building our house. I measured the outline of the structure and it complies with the original English requirement for first settler land ownership that the dwelling had to be an 18' by 20' seven stud structure. The other requirement was that the first settlers clear 5 acres of the woodland to English mowing hay within 5 years of settling the land. If the settler complied, then he could have title to the land free and clear. That was the basis of how our town got settled after its 1752 charter. The other clue to its original use as a first settler's cabin is the wear on the wellhead stone immediately to the south of the southern doorway. Generations of steps to fetch water have left an obvious wear pattern, which tells me the direction of use was coming from the cabin.

At some point after Peter Holbrook established title to the land on November 11, 1763, I believe that Peter Holbrook expanded his cabin by building the current house to the south of the Sugarhouse. It is highly likely that his family's growth in number of children demanded such a move. The original cabin then was converted to a barn-like shed and any windows would have been relocated to the new house. So goes our thinking.

When the Perrys acquired the house in the 1880's they converted the use of the cabin/barn/shed to house the fruits of their primary interest in logging and lumbering; hence, the opening for the saw rig and the storage of cut planks throughout the structure. The Perrys also used to sugar the enormous sugar maples that line the road. They converted the fireplace with a brick domed burn pit so they could "boil down" the sap. A living Perry family member gave me a sketch of what it looked like.

When my parents acquired the farm, the Sugarhouse was in pretty sad shape. They converted it to a summer outdoor cooking location where Dad would burn some neat 2-inch thick steaks. That's another story. The two ovens and the southern fireplace were pretty useless, as the mortar had begun to fail and some of the bricks had fallen in. My Mom wanted Dad to re-point them; however, Dad had many more important construction projects to attend to. He died in 1968 after a lengthy illness and the Sugarhouse was largely abandoned. However, the New Hampshire winters and weather did not let up. Some time in the 1970's, the entire structure pancaked on top of the fireplace. Over the ensuing years, Mom and I would pull the timbers away and eventually we were left with a rather large pile of bricks piled on top of a collapsed mantel at half-mast upon the two enormous hearthstones. So, it sat from the 1970's till mid 1990s.

In 1993, Louise designed the "new room" (our now living room) which tucks into the northeast corner of the old house, invisible from the road. This effort required digging up the ground for new concrete footings and such. This activity unearthed some neat artifacts from earlier days and a fresh supply of some really fine granite foundation and building stones. I piled most of them on the site of the old Sugarhouse. After we finished painting and staining the new room, we were able to enjoy the view north up the meadow. However, the sight of the old foundation area with all its rubble was not appealing. This fact gave us the incentive to change the view. Louise had always wanted a flower garden and a barbecue pit with two wing armatures for serving food and storage. I liked the idea of rebuilding the original fireplace but needed some time to warm up to the armature concept. Liz, Edmond, and I had attempted a simple small outdoor stone fireplace, which was too primitive in my opinion. So, a plan evolved to landscape the view and the new room. First, I built two stone walls in front of the doors of the new room against the foundation. Then I created a curving small stone wall in a crescent shape to house a raised day lily flowerbed. Once those were done, I began a long, tedious process to rebuild/restore the original fireplace. This process took about 4 years of weekends and may still be considered to be a work in progress. The most challenging step was to move the two 1,500 pound hearthstones 2 feet to the east so a new brick walkway could connect the two original threshold stones. Louise and I used metal pincer bars and inched them into place. We had fun leaving a small metal time capsule box with a few items from our era under the hearthstones,…oh my! Then I laid a frame of cinderblock in the shape of a "U." I filled the open blocks with stone and cement so they would last another 200 years. Then I faced the cinderblock with the original old bricks and some fieldstone for relief. I topped both armatures with bluestone slabs slightly tilted for weather run-off. Then I began building the large fireplace on the north side and allowed space for a barbecue on the south side.

During the fireplace construction phase, I was confronted by two very interesting dilemmas. The first was installing the original cooking crane. While digging up the entire site by hand, I had unearthed the original cooking crane. However, I wasn't sure how to attach it to the fireplace. After visiting Hawk's Mountain Ironworks in Springfield VT, I learned I needed to install two pinions....which I did. The hand-forged iron crane from the 1760's slipped into place.

The second challenge involved the original fireplace's granite mantel. Our "new room" construction crew attempted to sell me on the idea that it would make a good doorstep to the new room. I remained unconvinced. It seemed to me it should be returned to its former place of honor atop the new outdoor fireplace as its reborn mantel. I held firm. The mantel is hand cut granite 6 feet long and 8 by 10 inches thick.

I spent several nights trying to figure how I could lift it myself. Eventually I decided that a man needs to know his limitations, so I contracted with a neighbor to drive his tractor up to the farm and lift it into place with a strong chain. Good move!

FARM SETTLEMENT STRUCTURES

My theory of the farm settlement starts with what we called "The Sugarhouse" – likely the first settlers' original cabin. Additionally Peter Holbrook likely dug and lined the well, which sits immediately to the south of the cabin. The next likely structure would've been the main house, as it exists today without the wrap-around porch or the "L" at a right angle. The rest of the Holbrooks' energy had to be consumed with clearing the land for planting. This took several years of really hard labor. In all likelihood, the trees were used for winter fuel and the stumps, pulled out by oxen, were left to dry or be burned. In the process of clearing and pulling stumps, they became acquainted with New Hampshire's primary product......stones. These stones became the material with which to build the stone walls that outline the property. I am told that stone wall building ended in the 1840's with the arrival of barbed wire. So, the wall building period for the Holbrooks and Bennetts lasted from 1763 to around 1840, some 77 years. Leavenworth had nothing on building stone walls in Southern New Hampshire! I remain truly amazed whenever I think of the physical energy used for that effort.

There are/were additional structures that populated the farm; however, I can only guess at their date of arrival. The "L" seems to be a next logical addition some time later but during the time of oxen (before the use of horses). I say this because the "L" part of what we call the "Magic Shed" had two stalls, and I was told by the Perrys that they were used by the oxen. In fact, we still have two of the original ox bows that were used by these beasts of burden. The oxen were the equivalent of the modern bulldozer/backhoe. The farm could not have been built without them. The most important role among many was to help guide the massive foundation stones into place. I wish I had a record of the names of the oxen, as they were truly the unsung heroes of our farm and the entire town.

The oxen also were used to pull an ox cart, which was another essential to a first settler's site. That ox cart at our farm had its own shed located down "Old Bryant Road." This vestige of a road heads east into the woods. It is our opinion that "Old Bryant Road" may have been the original road to get to the farm. The Sugarhouse seems to orient to that old road rather than to the current road. The ox cart or its successor survived our arrival, but not beyond. I used it by hand to run/roll logs down from the meadow for firewood cutting. It was a two-wheeled vehicle with wheels which were about 5 feet in diameter. The ox shed foundation stones are still there; however, the rest of the structures have gone to dust in my lifetime.

The Carriage Barn was one of the finer structures in full decay when we arrived. This barn had two huge doors which swung open. The barn was adjacent but not attached to the "L." I suspect this separation might have been introduced to lessen damage in event of a fire. The barn was built over a slight hollow (now filled in where our current Garage Shed was placed). The foundation timbers were in full decay; however, most of the upper structure was still standing. The key to its demise was the wood-shingled roof that was in decay and leaked snow and rain. The crowning gem of the Carriage Barn was a real carriage. It was an old-time buggy carriage which would hold maybe 4 to 6 people. Herb and I would play cowboys and Indians there for hours. I can't tell you how many times this stagecoach was held up and robbed. Eventually several real young robbers stole it and ran it off the dirt road into the brook north of the house; that was its final demise. It had a small brass plate behind the rear seat indicating it was a Concord, New Hampshire product. The spare wheels had a use during our family's period. The wooden spokes were removed and used to hold up any window in the house.

Next south of the Carriage Barn, also detached, stood a fine "Corncrib" painted a weathered red and was half full of corn when we arrived in the 40's. This crib was sitting at a half-cocked angle and was fully open to the air to dry its contents. When I was 13, after receiving my first machete, I was encouraged to cut the brush growing up and around the farm. When I got to the north side of the corncrib, I spied a 4-foot sugar maple sapling. I raised my arm to dispatch it, and then I stopped. I raised it again and stopped. I thought to myself that this nice-looking sapling could be close to my age, and here I was going to kill it in the blink of an eye. I raised my arm the third time and stopped again. No, I just could not cut this guy. Someday he might be standing and that dumb corncrib would be gone. In fact, that is just what has happened. The sapling, which received the reprieve, is standing to this day as a 30-foot maple tree shadowing the new garage shed. When the new Amish-made Garage Shed arrived in 2003, I convinced the delivery people to jockey the shed around that former sapling.

A Perry family member tells me that a one-car garage stood next south; however, it was removed before we acquired the farm. The garage in question was removed to a nearby lake to be used as a boathouse there.

The remains of the multi-story red barn across the street from the house has a few interesting stories. When we arrived on the scene, it had become derelict. According to the Perrys, they were not able to get tin roofing material during World War I, and they therefore had to use inferior wooden shingles, which rotted and thus began the demise of this magnificent structure. Its primary purpose was to house some cows and some hay for the horses as well. My brother and I were forbidden from playing in and around the barn for fear of it collapsing as well as our stepping on rusty nails (which I had become quite good at).

The barn's two huge doors faced the north and could be seen through a meadow back then by our neighbor to the north. Mr. Willard was a hunter and had a practice every fall of "zeroing in" his 30-30 deer rifle by placing a white target on the doors of our barn and then firing from his back door. This only occurred once every fall; however, wouldn't you know, it happened one weekend after we arrived when the Willards didn't know we were at our farm. I had crossed the dirt road and was playing to the west of the old red barn when "Blam, Blam, Blam!" came the sound of the 30-30 roaring in the country air. I bolted for the safety of our farmhouse just in time to hear another "Blam, Blam, Blam!" After that incident, we always let the Willards know when we had arrived for the weekend!

One other interesting feature of the barn was an indoor silo in the northwest corner. This would house grain grown at the farm, I believe. When the farm was sold to us, the Perrys had already removed the timbers (2x4s) from the silo to build their chicken coops at their new home. The last items to be removed from the big red barn were the enormous red doors. My dad always liked them and thought he would use them someday. Dad was a product of the Depression; hence, the doors still reside in the "Magic Shed." I have since donated one of the doors for a dining room table project in Litchfield, CT. It seats ten folks I am told.

The last structures to be mentioned are the chicken coops. The Perrys were consummate chicken farmers. A string of simple wood and wire structures ran from the Sugarhouse northeast to Old Bryant Road. These were in sad shape when we arrived as well.

SATURDAY NIGHT LIVE

It was the summer of 1949 on a warm Saturday afternoon in July and our grungy work details around the farm had been shut down for the day. It was time to get ready to go to the big city a few miles away. Saturday night at the movies in the big city! What a rush that was for an 8 year old! I cannot recall just what my particular grungy work detail jobs entailed, but I did know I was as dirty as any boy my age and circumstance could be. Now normally that condition would require a nice hot bath with lots of soap and scrubbing. In our case, however, we didn't have any hot or running water.

Here was Mom's game plan: Pack some fresh underwear, shirts and jeans and load the family up in the car, and then stop for a bath on the way to town. Let me explain. On the route we took into town, there was a swimming hole north of the bridge that my parents had noticed. Mom's plan was to entice her two dirty little boys into the swimming hole for a cool dip and sneak a little soap along for the dirt removal. As I recall there was always a debate over how the soap would be applied, and to whom it would be applied. I do recall that the soap of the day was a dirty gray bar called "LAVA" which could remove anything and usually felt like sandpaper when applied. Once the bath was done, we'd towel off, change our clothes (hiding behind the car and road) and then we were good to go to town!

Back into the 1948 four-door Plymouth, and we would head towards town. As we approached a familiar pond, I'd always keep an eye out for airplanes, especially "float planes" which might make an appearance on the Pond. That was quite cool. The town was a commercial hub then as now; however, there were few automobiles even on a Saturday night in 1949. I also recall seeing a horse-drawn farm wagon with a family in the flatbed tie up near the theater, and then the kids, wearing straw hats, would all hop out for an evening on the town! We usually parked near the Diner on Main Street. In those days, Main Street was huge without any center divider. Parking was head in to the curb and railroad tracks crossed the center of Main Street.

The evening had its own sweet rituals with only slight variations which I will note. We'd park and then usually Mom had something at Woolworth's she would want to check out, while Dad and the boys would pile into the Army Navy Surplus store to view the war surplus and relive the War. Dad always had to pick up something. We would rejoin Mom while running on the squeaky wooden floors of the 5 and 10, and then we would window shop at the storefronts. We would then cross the street and check out what was showing at the other theater in town, and then bolt for the "News Stand" near the railroad tracks. Herb and I would race to see who could get to the comic book rack first. The "News Stand" had the most complete collection of comics a kid's heart could desire. Dad would always buy the evening newspaper.

If we were real lucky we'd hit this location close to the time the Boston and Maine train from Boston arrived. What a sight to see the steel beast approach and cross Main Street next to the "News Stand." To me, trains were a big deal, because any time Dad came from or went somewhere special, he took the train. Mom, of course, would admonish us to look out for the train and not get too close, God bless her! The train depot was just west of the "News Stand."

The next thrill in our ritual was a trip to the candy store! This was the epicenter for a young boy, right up there with movie houses. The shop was next to the theater, and you had to climb up a short number of stairs to the front door. The front window had a huge metal bowl with a mixer rotating a vat of chocolate fudge. This dominated the window. As you entered the door, there was a smallish foyer with white windowpanes on the left displaying various candies behind glass in fancy boxes. To the right there was also some white trimmed glass which looked over the fudge-making work area. Straight ahead, there was a small open window for placing and paying for an order. The rules were always the same. We were allowed one choice of candy not to be eaten until the following day so our dinner appetite wasn't spoiled. Well....maybe a small taste, just one. My constant dilemma was whether to choose a heart of hard maple sugar or a smaller soft maple sugar soldier or Indian head....hmmm, which would it be, which would it be?!

Our purchases were always placed in a small white bag that had the name of the store printed in black. Dad always bought some black licorice and Mom would pick up a few white cream-filled sweet chocolates. Our next stop was back across the street to the Diner. That would include a hot dog for the boys and the "Saturday night special" for Mom and Dad. The object was to get out of the Diner with enough change for the movies! The Diner was a classic and I believe it still exists today; however, it no longer adorns Main Street.

Discussion at dinner revolved around which movie we would attend. There were three theaters in town, and we walked past them all to check out the show times and what might appeal, judging from the huge wall posters. Each theater seemed to attract a different audience: one would feature a western, one a sweeping romance, and another a crime/drama. Herb and I would always lobby for the theater with the western serials and then a full-length western or crime movie. Mom went for the romance and the drama and Dad liked the latest crime or western movie. Mom was usually, but not always, outvoted. There was a good chance that Herb and I could whine our way to the serial location next to the Diner. We loved it, but Mom and Dad....not so much. Those serials were awesome.....Tom Mix, Cisco Kid, Hopalong Cassidy, Lone Ranger, Roy Rogers and on and on. The serials always gave the kids an advantage in their argument to stay at a particular theater week after week. Kids and moviemakers were not stupid!

After the movie, we would find that the warm sticky summer day had turned cool and crisp and clear. The ride home was neat, gliding along looking at the mist in the meadows underneath the towering white pines which lined the roadway. As we wandered back up the dirt road towards the farm, we'd become "hunter alert" to catch a glimpse of any deer in our distant headlights path. Normally we'd see a couple and that was its own thrill. The last thrill of the night could happen as we pulled into the farmyard at night's end. The arch of the headlights would splash the porch and the maples in the front yard. All eyes were peeled for bright eyes looking back at us. The predators might be perched on a limb or perhaps the porch.....the dreaded Bobcats of "the Hill"!

Now that's Saturday Night Live!

LEARNING TO DRIVE THE COMET

This tale concerns New Year's weekend 1985. Daughter Kate was invited to a New Year's Eve party in Vermont with her then boyfriend. Mike was a camp romance from the prior summer and I could tell Kate very much wanted to go. Logistics were the issue as it happens for almost any 15-year-old with an out-of-state invitation. How to get there? That's where I came in....."perhaps you could drive me to the party in Vermont?.....oh please, please, please, pretty please!" We were living in Connecticut at the time and the farm had been shut down for the winter. Kate had this kind invitation from Mike and his Mom that included chaperoned lodging at their home. After much reflection, I recalled how special these times were at age 15 and decided to help out as best I could.

I really had two dilemmas: the first was wheels and the second was my own lodging, as I hadn't been part of the invite. The first was solvable as long as there was no messy weather. We had a second, antique car.....a 1960 Comet Convertible with a broken heater, a leaking canvas top (truly a Rag Top) and very bald no-tread tires.....but it did run and was perhaps capable for the task at hand. The second issue was lodging, and perhaps I could manage to "camp out" at the farm, even though the water had been drained and the heater had not

43

yet been installed. So, the only heat possible was from a wood stove in the kitchen which was rated at 25 minutes per fill up of wood!

"Please, please, please, pretty please" again rang in my ear as I ruminated on the situation. My plans for New Year's Eve were quite nil that year, so the prospect of an overnight adventure had some appeal. I had negotiated other weekends in the Adirondacks with more hostile environmental elements. Camping at the farm should be a piece of cake by comparison to a few Adirondack winter camping trips. So Dad eventually consented to solving the logistics of Kate's plan some time before he thoroughly thought through the details of his logistics.

The weekend came, and much discussion took place over what Kate would wear and various packing needs. I tried to get a bead on the weather for that weekend and only had marginal info with a possible snowfall sometime over the weekend. Off we went....Vermont party or Bust! We arrived in good form and Mike's Mom was a delightful hostess. I dropped my cargo off and felt she was in good hands. I turned the Comet east and wandered to the farm. It was a cold early-winter day, sunny and bright with no snow on the ground.....so far so good.

I pulled into the farmyard and unpacked my camping gear. The house was extremely chilly, so my first task was to stoke up the wood stove and turn on the electric oven and leave the door of the oven open while I unpacked. This was an old Adirondack trick I had heard about. I closed all the doors except the bedroom and the kitchen. I was reasonably comfortable in about an hour. The daylight was fading as I made some noodle concoction over the stove. I didn't have any radio, or TV, or Internet back then, so sack time came early. Sweet youth.

I think I had slept about 1 hour when I awoke in my sleeping bag because my nose was quite cold. After a few moments of denial, I got up and attended the kitchen wood stove and then dozed off again. My nose alarm went off every 45 to 60 minutes all night...each time the stove gods had to be fed. Daylight was a relief, as were a hot cup of instant coffee and stale donuts. Mid-day I set out for Vermont, knowing that the partygoers were still getting their beauty rest.

I picked up a sleepy Kate and headed back to the farm. Details of the prior evening were slim to non-existent, but I could tell a good time had been had by all....Dads just know those things. It was a very cold and dark New Year's Day as we departed Vermont. By the time we crossed the river a light snow had begun to fall. It was just beautiful as it drifted down so silently. The evergreens along the river were dusted with snow. The magic of the day was underscored. The dirt road to the farm was firm and clear as we pulled onto our road. We eased down "Hallas Hill" without giving it or the tires a thought. We pulled into the farmyard and went into the house. The 24 hours of stove wood burning gave a warmth and pleasant smell as we sat down for a late lunch of whatever.

As I finished lunch, I looked out the window and noticed that the light snow had turned heavier and the accumulation was now about a half inch on the grass and the road. A light bulb went off in my head that maybe the bald tires would have a difficult time assisting us in getting back up "Hallas Hill." Our plan had been to spend the night, but I began to think that if we didn't make it out right then, we might be stuck for several days, as the Comet would never make it up the hill in several inches. I told Kate to repack and we scrambled to assemble the camping supplies and piled it all back into the Rag Top.

I pulled out onto the dirt road, which now had a good inch of snow, and I drove the Comet down to the brook and up the bottom of the Hill. I got about a third of the way up the hill before the wheels began to spin and the car lost enough steam to make it. I backed down the hill as Kate asked, "Dad, are we going to make it out?" Her composure was beginning to slip and I was hiding mine, as only parents of teenagers know how to do. I backed down to the brook and then gunned the Comet up the hill. This time I got close to the true crest, merely feet or inches from success and then the wheels spun and the car slipped sideways. Ugh! My mind raced to consider any options to solve this dilemma....no chains, no spare tires, no snowplows! The hill was too big to shovel, with no salt or sand that wasn't covered in frost....and on and on. I was soooo close I could smell success at the crest of the hill. I had to try something different. I needed more traction! That was the deal! I stopped the car and popped the trunk open, went over to the stone wall and loaded several hundred pounds of boulders into the trunk. Kate looked at me as if I were Looney Tunes. I backed down and tried again. I inched a few feet further as the traction idea was working, but I still needed just a tad more. I just needed a push, but how could I push and drive the car at the same time? BINGO! Have Kate drive and I would push! It sounded cool to me, but was very, very scary to Kate. She had never driven a car before in her life, let alone on bald tires, on a dirt road, in a leaky Rag Top.........."geeez Dad, how could you?" I pleaded that she could do it, and I would coach her. She merely needed to do what I told her; otherwise, we would likely freeze to death in a cold farmhouse. That argument worked....it wasn't subtle, but it worked!

She got into the driver's seat. I showed her the pedals and told her all she needed to do was to get the car beyond the crest of the hill. Then she would be done and I would take it from there. I explained that I would be pushing down on the back of car as she gassed it, and we'd get unstuck. That was the plan, Stan! I told her once more she could do this and we'd be home free. She eased the gas as I had told her as I pressed hard on the trunk and dug my boots into the dirt road. The tires moved and began to spin, but I had guessed correctly as we continued to move slowly up to the crest and beyond. Success!

We cleared the crest and I yelled at Kate to stop the car. She yelled back "How do I stop the car, Dad?" I yelled, "Take your foot off the gas." The car slid to a stop. I hugged my daughter when she took the passenger side. As we drove off, I turned to her and said "Kate you just passed your driver's test with flying colors! Well done!" I could see the pride in her beautiful smile.

Learning the "Trades" at the Farm

Elizabeth McClure Hallas; a/k/a Betsy, Bets, "Tugger," Lizzie, Liz and then Liz Hallas, Restoration Architect!? How did that last item come to happen? I believe it all started at our 1763 first settlers' farm!

Perhaps the most telling and iconic image of "Tugger" shows her on the front porch, age 2 or 3, sitting Indian style with a hammer and nail in her small hands. She is about to hammer a nail into a wooden stay from a pine bucket with a number 10 stainless aluminum nail......a sure sign of things to come in her life! She looked so serious and intent on the task at hand. All construction training starts with a hammer and a nail!

Next came "how to build a fireplace" without mortar. I had a trial run at building an outdoor fireplace at the current site of the "Pit"; the former location of a cabin/Sugarhouse. I had cleared the fallen bricks away and had a patch of foundation stones and a large hearth stone. One weekend Liz and cousin Edmond assisted me in assembling many of these heavy stones into an outdoor fireplace site, Adirondack style. Upon completion, a barefooted Liz stood on the finished project, arm raised in victory with her fist clenched and a beautiful smile on her face. What's next Dad?

My father always told me the most important thing about maintaining and restoring old houses is to protect the roof, especially in snowy New Hampshire. I recall working at his side while he pounded nails while re-roofing the wrap-around porch. This was a tricky job because of the slight pitch and elbow connection to the main roof angle. I recall being hollered at for walking on that joint. Well, in the mid to late 80's, I needed to re-do the same wrap-around roof, as time and winters had taken their toll. I decided to include Liz in this exercise as a "roofer's assistant." She was game, much to my surprise. I decided to lay a shingle-style roof rather than a rolled tarpaper style that had been the material to date. This required pounding many roofing nails, as this porch roof is quite large. As I recall, Liz did about thirty to forty percent of the nail pounding and loved every minute of it (or so I recall). Liz checked off "Roofer's Assistant" in her trade's manual.

Well, Dad....what about the frame construction and roof raising trades? My log cabin in the woods provided the perfect opportunity for such lessons. (See the tale on "Cabin Fever") Liz had observed my obsession with cutting 41 logs for the Adirondack style lean-to. I believe she assisted in helping me skin a few and pile them in place to cure. Louise and I had managed to build the floor of the cabin and frame the walls up to head level with Louise skinning the logs and chinking between the logs while I continued to cut down more trees, but then the project turned difficult. I needed to raise the beams to hold the roof rafters, lay the roof rafters, and then put down the under-sheaf of plywood to hold the tin roof panels. No way could I do this alone.

Liz had been an able roofer's assistant, so why not become a "Carpenter's Assistant"? She was game even though neither of us really knew what we were doing. I had helped a friend raise his roof in the Adirondacks, so I had a vague idea.

Liz and her friend, Erik, spent the weekend at the farm with us, and I pressed them into service. We spent one complete and successful Saturday placing the beams, raising the rafters, and laying the plywood! Liz graduated to yet another trade rank! And so it went.

Eventually she put it all together and became the Restoration Architect she is today! And it all started on the floor of the porch at the farm!

A THOUSAND WORDS ARE WORTH A PICTURE?

First, there is a perfectly classic photo shot of Betsy and Kate by the woodpile. Kate is astride the wood bucking saw horse with one arm raised as if to say, "Hi there world!" while sister Betsy is sitting on a log stump wearing bib overalls with a book in one hand and her hand on her knee smiling into the camera, nice green ferns flank one side and a pile of lumber the other side.....a study of sisters in summer.

Then there is "sisters in the hammock": the two of them sitting in the old red and white striped hammock from my childhood. Unlike my brother and I who fought in and about the hammock, the sisters seem to be at peace, at least for the photo moment!

The next classic photo group is the series on Trout fishing! Betsy is holding the green "Old Pal" worm can (I don't think she knew what it was yet) and Kate is obliging Dad, holding her Dad's father's fishing rod and woven trout creel prior to the day's adventure. Unfortunately, trout fishing never became an esteemed activity for the girls; perhaps the worms or handling the fish got in the way!

Fourth of July, 1976 was a day to be remembered at the farm in photos and readings. The girls were quiet as Dad read the Declaration of Independence and rang the bell at 2 p.m. I have a lovely photo of the girls and their cousin standing in front of our flag-draped porch, each with their hands across their hearts. Later in the day, the girls were caught waving their flags and wearing their Indian Princess vests while watching the Richmond Fourth of July parade in town.

The funniest picture ever taken during their childhood took place at the farm. Kate and Betsy were playing "cowgirl dress up"! I don't know where they got the idea to get into their getup, but it is truly hysterical. Betsy is wearing my mother's hip boots and her white summer three quarter, light coat, Dad's construction gloves and my mother's mother's huge, wide-brim straw hat, pointing one of my cap guns at me with a truly wacky smirk on her face. Kate was fully dressed in my Uncle Henry's World War II rain suit and was using both hands to hold up the pants. She wore the classic Southern New Hampshire woven straw worker's hat with a beautiful toothy grin and flowing blond hair. WOW, what a shot! It always brings a smile to my heart.

Then there are the winter shots; first, the sisters on cross country skis, up in the snowy meadow on an early spring day, each holding poles and turning back to smile at the camera. Also, a very charming shot of Betsy standing next to a sugar maple tree next to a sap bucket in the front yard with the farm in the background and our Ford Pinto station wagon's front wheel fender within the frame.

I also have a nice series of photos of the girls at the State Fish Hatchery. They show the girls intently looking at the breeding pools full of beautiful baby trout. The State no longer uses that facility and the pools have since been filled in.

And finally, another humorous shot of Liz in the fall. The leaves are off the trees and clearly, it is a very chilly day at the farm. Again as a Dad, I worried about hunters wandering the woods, and so I directed the girls to wear bright red or yellow when out in the yard and in the woods (standard New Hampshire practice during hunting season.) I had parked my Jeep in the front yard to unpack for the weekend, and as I got ready to back it out and park across the road, Liz decided she should play "traffic cop." So, she moved into the deserted dirt road wearing a red bib and white mittens and pretending to stop non-existent traffic on the road while waving me to back up......way too funny! Such are the images of youthful days at the farm.

The Lost Art of Driving on New Hampshire Dirt Roads

Who cares about the lost art of driving on New Hampshire dirt roads? Here is why you should!

Louise and I had decided to take a break one January in 2003 and to take a drive up to the farm to breathe in the winter beauty of the forest after a snowfall. It was early January and it had snowed a quarter inch of powder on the frozen dirt road. As we passed our friends' farm down the road from ours, I noticed a truck with a rear cab barreling around a curve in the distance. I quickly estimated that his speed was too much for the conditions and the terrain he was coming into. His light gray older truck seemed to levitate towards us. We were driving our brand new Jeep Grand Cherokee, candy apple red, my pride and joy.

My immediate mental calculation was to get as far off the road as I could go, as I suspected the oncoming vehicle would soon be completely out of control given his speed and the quarter inch of new snow on frozen dirt. It was just as I suspected! The problem was that the road was 13 feet wide with enormous snow banks on each side! I quickly turned the steering wheel and gunned the Jeep into the three foot frozen snow bank as far as the engine would propel it and then waited for impact from the approaching gray ghost.

It seemed like forever, but he skidded towards us and there was not enough room for his width and mine to share the 13-foot snow-covered runway. His left front corner headlight creased my left front side panel near the headlight. He came to rest window to window having crushed each of my three left panels.......not good. I had yelled to Louise to hang on and then said a quick prayer. The prayer was answered as the offender sideswiped us and had not hit us head on, thank God. If the snow bank were smaller, or not there, I could have evaded him totally, but that was not to be.

To add insult to injury, the offending driver was not insured, apparently not required by New Hampshire motor vehicle laws. I knew the damage was substantial and insisted that we remain in place until the Police were called. A State Policeman eventually arrived and looked at his New Hampshire license plate and my Connecticut license plate and determined instantly that I had not properly shared the road, all 13 feet of it. Apparently, speed and road conditions did not matter. The art of driving on dirt roads in New Hampshire had been lost on this officer of the law! (I would love to send this to him.) Net, net....the repair bill came to over $5,000 and our insurance had to cover it with an increase in our insurance rates. The irresponsible offender got off scot-free!

So how did I come by the now lost art of driving on dirt roads in New Hampshire? Believe it or not, my father made sure that my brother and I were clued in during the early 1940's on these very same dirt roads. It would be years before we acquired our licenses. My earliest recall happened just up the hill from the farm where there is a spring, which runs in the Spring (under and next to the road) leaving the shoulders quite treacherous. My mother had pulled over too far one Spring when approached by an oncoming vehicle and the right wheels sunk to above the hubcaps! So the first rule is never assume a friendly shoulder! Instead, slow down and begin the lost art of negotiated passing.

The second rule is that you and the oncoming vehicle share the road, all 13 feet! So passing without slowing down is not smart or readily possible as is the case with paved roads and other towns, which may have wider dirt roads. A quick visual of the dirt roads in our neck of the woods shows only two worn tire lines and a center dirt path. This second rule reinforces the necessity to moderate your speed and reinforces the benefit of visual intelligence concerning conditions and environment.

The interesting result of the first two rules is that you quickly realize that we are all in this together once one is on a dirt road of modest proportions. Much is to be gained by empathy and compassion for one's fellow traveler. On the other hand, much is to be lost if either chooses to ignore the mutual impacts (pun intended). This mutually beneficial conduct then leads to a new level of respect and rapport with one's fellow travelers. You meet on some lonely stretch of back road; you each slow down and take measure of the prevailing conditions before deciding what further path to take. Interestingly, some folk, well experienced in this lost art, will attempt to anticipate a solution early by pulling over at a wide point or perhaps backing up to a wide point. It doesn't happen very much anymore, but it is delightful when it does.

There also is a tip of the hat or a friendly wave rather than current day road rage over a lost advantage. On a warm summer day even a pleasant hello is exchanged.

Oh, how times have changed!

2

❀ ❀ ❀

Farm History
Holbrook & Perry Era
(1760's – 1920's)

NEW HAMPSHIRE LETTER #1

June 8, 1993

Dear Herb, Kate, and Liz,

This spring and summer have been an extraordinary time of discovery regarding our New Hampshire property. The reasons for this are varied. First, Louise and I have nearly completed a legal title search at the Cheshire County Registry of Deeds. Second, the heavy snow this winter has created a tremendous amount of ground shadows from its weight, i.e., the old wagon wheel trails are reflected by the compression of the old wheel marks vs. the non-marked areas. Louise and I have also been rereading an 1880 History Book on our Town, and lastly, discussions with Lewis who lives in the farm at the bottom of the hill. On top of these factors, Louise and I have been discussing, debating, and theorizing! Where to begin? Well I guess I will list the new facts/ideas and give a reference comment to support it. Here goes.

1. First Settler, Owner, and Builder of the House

All things point to Peter Holbrook with a deed dated Nov.11, 1763. He was born in 1740; first seen in town in 1762; attended the first town meeting in

1765; fought in the Revolutionary War in 1777; marched to the defense of Fort Ticonderoga as part of a relief effort since Colonials were under tremendous pressure from British troops coming down from Canada! Peter sold house & farm to George Buffum in 1794 for 260 pounds, 10 shillings....we have read the original deed! Peter came from Uxbridge Mass. along with others. A large number of early settlers were from Uxbridge, Mass., Smithfield, RI., and Cumberland, RI. This is particularly fascinating since our grandfather on our father's side came from Galicia (near the Ukraine) and also first entered America at Cumberland in 1909. What this tells me is that the patterns of immigration from England and then Eastern Europe followed established patterns which repeated themselves for generations. It is kind of spooky to think that Dad, like Peter Holbrook, had roots in the Blackstone River valley. We also read that Peter Holbrook signed the "Oath of Association" in 1776 (Oath of loyalty to those opposed to the King). In 1795/96, Peter and Lydia moved off the mountain to a farm a town away. He died there in 1806 and is buried in the local cemetery.

2. Roads and Cellar Holes Found!

According to Lewis, the dirt road down the hill to his farm was laid out in 1848. The road which goes east/west and is abandoned at the north side of the next farm was a busy road until 1848. The way to get to the Perry farm was east on this road and then left down the hill, the way we went as kids. This was part of an old county road, which later became abandoned by the town in favor of the existing dirt road down the hill. We have found old carriage trail evidence that a road ran from behind Deveda's farm with periodic spurs leading to the farms now on our road. I want to map this old road. I have part of it mapped from hikes this spring....I'll show you when we get together. Louise and I hiked back to the "Cattle Pound" at the Old Bryant Place. We used to call this area where all the roads came together "42nd Street" (coined by my Dad). While reading the 1930's manuscript, I found a reference to the dimensions of a "Town Pound" which exactly fits this structure. I need to re-measure it to be sure! I also have a theory regarding the stone wall that runs east. One side of the walled lane goes due east and the other curves to the south as if to operate as a "catcher"....perhaps of sheep or cattle. The curve in the wall relates to another even older cellar hole slightly east and south which contained a grazing meadow, I believe.

3. Old Wagon Trails

I have seen many wagon trail marks this spring. Many of them seem to have come down the hill by the brook, crossed the brook, and then split into at least three or four directions! I believe (but have no proof) they come from a period before the Old Bryant Road. All of them have big trees growing in them. The mystery is which came first, the old wagon tracks or the stone walls? Lewis tells me that the stone walls were constructed between 1762 and the 1830's. Several of the trails seem to lead to the old school house just north on the other side of our road. We did find one that follows the brook on the north side and then lines up with the Old Bryant Road. All of this was a new discovery this year, thanks to the snows of 1993.

4. Our House, New Discovery

When the clapboards were removed to construct the new room, we found newspaper that had been used as insulation. The newspapers were dated 1906 which suggests, but doesn't confirm, that the porches were put on then. Vince and John (our contractors) dug up a spoon and several horseshoes. We also uncovered pieces of various old wallpaper patterns from prior generations, and we rediscovered a small well (6 feet deep) east of the house in the swale. We have a theory that that well was used while Peter Holbrook built the original cabin.

Many mysteries remain!

NEW HAMPSHIRE LETTER #2

November 3, 1993

Dear Herb, Kate, and Liz,

This letter is being written to capture some of the rich and varied oral history of "Blueberry Meadow Farm." I am not sure where this will all go; however, I fear the tapestry will be lost unless it becomes recorded. I feel a responsibility to capture it by committing to disk/paper! The year 1993 literally unearthed a wealth of discovery for us. I have already written some of the historical material; however, some interesting oral history has come our way and I would like to leave footprints. Here goes!

Tales from Ernest as Told to Louise and Hank

Apparently, Ernest's grandfather Byron was approached by his wife Carrie to knock a door through the southeast room in the "L" to allow same floor access to the privy. He objected, stalled, and delayed over the years. Finally, after many years of debate etc., he knocked the doorway through for Carrie. Byron, however, would never use it; rather, he continued going outside into the shed up the stairs or out the door in the fireplace room down the stairs, around a corner then back up the stairs to the privy. Obviously, it took awhile for indoor plumbing to become accepted. (Or was it New Hampshire obstinacy?)

Along this line, Ernest shared another Byron story. Apparently, when Carrie was pregnant with Arthur (Ernest's father) she wanted to get some children's clothing patterns from Nahum, who lived on the east side of town many miles away. Exasperated, Carrie finally walked up to Byron and said "I want to get those patterns now!" Byron hitched up the wagon, got Carrie into the wagon and off they went; however, Byron walked by the wagon....he wouldn't get in; rather, he hoofed it all the way over and back!

Ernest shared that the garage had a slit trench dug under it so one could work under the Model "T" standing up....Yankee ingenuity.

The "Magic Shed" had an ox-lift built into it so the re-shoeing could be done without the ox leaning on the shoe man.

The scallop trim, so distinctive on the house, was hand sawn by Byron one winter. When John and Vince added new sections to the "new room," They both used a power saw device and felt that the scallop trim was very difficult to reproduce. They couldn't imagine the patience required to do the job entirely by hand. I added some spare pieces to the "Blueberry Meadow Farm" sign done during the blizzard of 1993!

When I showed Ernest a piece of column corner I saved from the elements at the old Taylor Place, next west of us across the beaver dam, he told us a few interesting stories. Apparently, you could see the Taylor House (originally the Thayer first settler's site) from the front porch over the tops of smaller trees. Lillian Randall had previously told us that she remembered seeing the farmhouse and lilacs growing there looking due west from our porch.

According to Ernest, one day the local sheriff arrived at the farm and inquired about what had happened to the Taylor place, that it had been vandalized and much of it torn down. Arthur turned to the sheriff and his companion and said: "Why, Mr. X got permission from the owner to remove the wood." Apparently, the sheriff's companion turned and said, "Why yes, I'd forgotten that. I did give him permission."

(Case closed)

According to Ernest, the small water wheel was a toy belonging to his father, built by his father. I suspect a child could not have done this, and that it was really done by Byron. Byron strikes me as a very interesting man the more I learn about him.

Ernest told Louise that the "Beehive Oven" was removed from the kitchen in favor of a cast Iron stove. He told me that the "L" had a summer kitchen with a small chimney along the east wall between the windows. I remember seeing that when we took possession of the farm in 1947.

I asked Ernest what kind of farm his father ran. He said that it was a subsistence farm. He cut wood, raised cows, and delivered cream to the town center twice a week. I remember my Dad saying that the lot across the street to the west was planted with potatoes. Ernest remembers a wood lot on the other side of the beaver dam to the west. He also confirmed a battery operated telephone system between our house, the Taylor farm and beyond. This was all installed in the late 1930's.

Ernest said that neither he nor his brother lived at the farm; only his father and his grandfather, Byron.

Ernest said they had to blast into rock in order to get to more water in the oldest well site outside of the new room.

I admired the neat brass oil lamps on the 1914 Model "T" (originally purchased at the farm by Byron) that he had driven back up to the farm. He said that in The "Big City" you had to have them lit even when you were parked at night or you could be fined. Apparently, Arthur was called out of a jury meeting by a constable on patrol to comply with the law.

Map from Lewis

Lewis gave me a copy of a map dated 1807. It indicates the present location of "Blueberry Meadow Farm" as "a large area under cultivation." It also refers to the brook as Buffum Brook!

NEW HAMPSHIRE LETTER #3

January 1995

Dear Herb, Kate, and Liz,

Over the past 12 months, additional information has been discovered regarding "Blueberry Meadow Farm." I felt it is significant enough to capture on disk/paper for the "information highway."

1. New Information Regarding Fire Site Deep in the Woods

During the spring of 1994 I was wandering out past the "Old Bryant Place" a mile or so east of the farm. I took a farm path/road to the northwest, which then bent west as it eased north. The trail crossed two stone wall openings and seemed to end up in a wet area northwest of the Bryant cellar hole on higher ground. Dry land was found further to the northwest of the location, so I wandered further up the hill. I had walked about 100/200 yards when I stumbled on what looked like a low barbecue pit. It had two sides, each outlined by slabs of granite 6 feet long and 10 x 8 inches. The south-pointing end had a head stone like a fireback, and the north-facing end was open. I found charcoal/wood remains inside as well as a scattering of bricks outside. There were no roads or paths visible. The fire site was ringed by small stones/boulders as if to hold a tent in place. This ring of stones was also observed by Louise's childhood friend, Sandy, who was present with us at a second inspection.

Several theories were expounded:

a. hunter's blind

b. Indian lodge site

c. site to cook large game

d. burial site (Indian or perhaps a diseased settler).

Each theory was hashed and rehashed. The troubling items were the presence of bricks and the lack of any clear path or trail. About a month ago, Lewis dropped off a booklet written in Vermont to acquaint landholders with the ability to identify sites discovered on their property. This booklet suggested yet another possibility which has since leaped into first place.....an old "sugaring off" site deep in the woods. Apparently, it was common to use a long fire pit with a brick arch using strong sides to hold large kettles to burn down the maple sap to syrup! The brick arch was also suggested to me in a sketch Ernest had made of such a layout in our "Sugarhouse." An old friend from Connecticut also confirmed this theory based on his childhood experiences in Maine. Finally, it does seem to make sense. Lewis and I, on a subsequent trip to the site stumbled across a depression in the ground close by that suggests that perhaps a shed had once existed there. It needs to be re-inspected for more evidence.

2. The Erratic Cave

About 50 to 75 yards north of the site described above there is a huge "Erratic." It is about the size of a large garage and appears to have broken off its base. The boulders sit pretty much on the top of the hill. The cleavage between the base and the upper "Erratic" created a cave about 30 feet long with excellent cover from the elements. A man crouching can enter from the north; however, he would have to crawl to exit the south end. A shelf located above the cave, which has an overhang, shows evidence of prior fire smoke stains on the east wall. All in all, it is a very interesting spot!

3. "Doors"

Early in January, Louise and I had the pleasure of dining at Lewis's. While touring the house, Priscilla commented that the front door was made by the Taylors at the mill at the top of the hill. The door is extremely wide, enough to fit a coffin through. The door style and age is identical to our front door at the farm.

4. Dams and More Dams

While dining with Lewis, he shared the fact that Arthur Perry (the man my parents purchased the farm from) used to work at the Mill at the bottom of the hill across the street from Lewis and Priscilla's farm. At night he would walk back up the hill, and he would close the water gate hole in the dam above the mill to build a headwater overnight. He would reopen it when he returned to work in the morning. Human-aided waterpower!

I took Lewis down to the cabin west of our farm to show him the telephone pole (more on that later). I took him along the brook coming back to the house and showed him the rock structure just below the first beaver dam halfway back to the road. I've suspected it was originally part of a water dam system for the mills below.

5. The Richmond Telephone and Telegraph System

Ernest had told me about the telephone and telegraph system that was used in town prior to the arrival of electricity. The only evidence I had found was the wire in the tree in the middle of the beaver dam, the battery pieces near the house, and the insulator in the ceiling of the basement.

I wanted to clear dead limbs off the stone wall near the cabin down at the beaver dam, so I picked up a large pole leaning on the wall. I discovered it was a telephone pole complete with a small cross arm to hold the insulators. I have moved it to a dry cover area above the cabin porch.

6. "Lots and Ranges"

One of the curiosities Louise and I observed in the title search concerned the discrepancies between various "Lots and Ranges" in regard to our farm specifically, but probably also applicable to other first settlers' farms. The starting point of confusion starts with the Town History text. The text contains a biographical sketch and includes reference to Peter Holbrook on one lot and range. However, the index in the back of the text refers to Peter at another lot and range. At this point, I found myself in a quandary, since the actual house referenced in the index as being succeeded by the Perrys is located on yet another lot and range.

This inconsistency has become troubling when we try to establish who lived in several cellar holes which are found in adjacent lots and ranges. For example, our second settler is referenced at one lot and range; however, that isn't located on any maps, and then he occupies our house, and then he moves to town and builds his final house. All of this results in puzzles, and pieces seemingly out of place. I'd really like to anchor the first settlers and then be able to understand the comings and goings and successions in our area.

The key to doing this came to my attention last weekend. I decided to reread the deed from "Blanchard to Peter Holbrook" which marks the formal official papers documenting the deeding out to our first settler, Peter Holbrook. There in plain English it states that Peter bought three lots and ranges running north-south with the correct lot and range numbers....Clear evidence of what and where he bought! And it fits the physical evidence, the house, the maps etc. Very interesting, very interesting!

NEW HAMPSHIRE LETTER #4

July 3, 1995

Dear Herb, Kate, and Liz,

This letter picks up from where the last one left off. I had several adventures this spring which I have been meaning to get down on paper. Here goes.

"The Old Carriage Road"

Sometime in March/April of this year, Lewis and I attempted to follow an old carriage road which I had stumbled across the prior year. We drove over to a road located due east of us on the other side of the mountain. We parked and hiked around the Aldrich cellar hole, which is about 200 to 300 yards down that road where it first becomes impassable. The Aldrich cellar hole is impressive....a wide highway, nice stone walls, large old maple trees. The cellar hole is on the left-hand side as you walk north on the road.

If you stand on the south side of the cellar hole facing south, you face a large yard area immediately to the south. Head for the southwest corner of this yard and then west....you should see a trail, wandering uphill to the west. If you look to the horizon you will notice a gap in the mountain to the west. This is where the carriage trail heads to the south side of this gap with a smallish brook to your right slightly out of sight. After a few hundred yards, it seems to look like an "old carriage road," hence the name.

Lewis and I are trying to find out whether this "old carriage road" actually climbs the mountain and connects to other cellar holes we've found up on top of the mountain. After a very long climb, the road follows the terrain and snakes west, then south, then west, then south several times. The road is very clear for about a half mile; then it seems unclear. As you near the crest of the mountain range, there are several terraces and rock outcrops which made the "road reading" very tricky. There are several places where the road looks like it would go around both sides of a large outcrop. I'd say we were successful in following it about three quarters of the way up the mountain; however, the final quarter was not very easy. The last quarter suggests that it would have been easier on a carriage than the first three quarters of the road. Our conclusion would be that the path likely was an old carriage road that linked one side of the mountain to the other. There are several large and beautiful rock outcrops, which were lush and green, a very lovely place to hike.

I believe the very early settlers would use the "old carriage road" to connect the two settlements on either side of the mountain; however, the eventual road our farm is on became more permanent, more reliable and easier to traverse during most seasons than the old carriage road. A form of transportation, "survival of the fittest."

An Attempt to Connect the Calvin Bryant Place with Lewis's Farm

Lewis and I took another ramble to see if we could connect his farm with the Old Bryant Place. We first followed the road east from behind the house just north of ours. About three quarters of the way down hill, just past where a path joins in from his farm, you will find a log transfer clearing probably 30x30 yards. If you go into that transfer clearing and head due east you will find a cellar hole about 50 yards in. It is obscured now due to heavy under brush; however, there is a large-sized boulder which provides a clue to its location. The boulder is an erratic, the size of a large truck. I believe this is the cellar hole of Jairus Perry and it resides in the next town, so you won't get any clues from old maps of our town. Lewis and I wandered around the stone walls and eventually took a main logging road running due east. It has spurs which flare to the south, up towards the hill. It is now my belief that the first spur is the old connecting road. However, in 1995 we didn't know that. We wandered about a quarter mile and then took a spur up the hill to the south. We did find the Town Line marker. (A big red stake.) We then returned east along the logging road and went about a half mile more, then turned south again up the hill to the top/crest. This last area was heavily logged; however, we didn't find the connecting road and had no new clues.

Once again, we wandered to the south and slightly westward, eventually coming back to the Old Bryant Place. This ended the exploration for 1995.

Continued Search for the Connecting Road 1996

I continued the search with a ramble by myself in 1996. I retraced the prior year's steps; however, I took the first spur from the J. Perry cellar hole, to the south and up the hill. It led me to the corner marker with the red stake. I continued to worm my way up and I seemed to find road-like marks, but none completely clear. I suspect time and the logging have dismantled the old roadbed. When I got to the top, I wandered to the right (westward) following the terrain of the crest. Eventually I got over to the cave rock, the erratic with a cave and signs of use from days gone by. I then circled back to the Old Bryant Road and headed north. About 100 yards north, I came to a wet area, where I circled to the left of it and then continued 20 to 40 yards to the north. Near this area I came across a pile of stones which I believe mark one or more of the following:

a. The original corner of the town (since the red stake is 100 yards away);

b. A watershed marker, as the water there runs both north and south;

c. An original lot and range marker for our town (most likely).

Take your pick. I want to take Lewis up there to check it out. The view from the crest of the Lake is exactly as I remember it as a kid of 13, when I used this route to go from the Bryant Place to the Perry farm. I returned home with an exhausted dog (Cody) who was so beat he almost collapsed. This was the last major hike I took him on.

"Old Carriage Road to the Pond" 1997

Lewis and I took a ramble and located the abandoned road that runs from our favorite swimming spot north to our farm. Our trip started by driving to the radar tower in Lewis's Gator. We retraced our steps from the prior year and then detoured over to the view to the east. On the way back towards the mountaintop, we took a left onto a new/old road that has been recently cleared. This trail heads south and is quite near the path that leads to the overlook. As we followed it south, we saw that it seemed to tie to an older road to the right. We diverted a few hundred yards to the southwest and found the Robinson's original cellar hole near a towering white pine. Another way to find it is to start at the radar tower area and follow the access road south back towards our road.

After visiting the Robinson cellar hole, we returned to the "old road" to the south. We continued south on that roadbed until we came to a "T" intersection near the (east/west) power lines. We took a left and headed east. That trail/road leads to the rear of the

78

original Newell House. After checking a small pond north of the farmhouse, we retraced our step to the "T" intersection. If you continue west at the "T," you will arrive at a meadow above an old Bolles site. Near the meadow on the east we intersected the old access road, and we took a right back on the access road to return to the Gator. About halfway up that road, we went north off it. At this location, we found remnants of the same old abandoned road we have hiked pieces of before. If we had continued north on this piece, we would have connected with the old road behind us. I am sure that this is the original old connecting road which is referenced in the history books. It is a great find and a fun exploration.

Eventually we retraced our steps to the access road and returned to the Gator. We explored the mounds found to the west. Local legend holds that these mounds were originally an old Indian burial site. I am not sure if that is fact or fiction.

3

❀ ❀ ❀

Special People
& Critters

FIRST "CRUSH"

Her name was Emily. She was my first and only New Hampshire "crush." I first met Emily when I was 14 or 15 years old during the summer vacation period. Emily and her older sister, Jane, lived down the hill northward on the dirt road we used to always take to go to town or to the lake. My brother Herb and I were very fond of these two gals. The family had another older brother named Holbrook, who was already up and out of the household when Herb and I came on the scene.

Both sisters were very pretty, full of that special New Hampshire energy, quick to laugh, athletic and very self-reliant (another great New Hampshire trait). My memory on meeting them is cloudy. My best guess is that my parents and their parents were friends and acquaintances with mutual friends who had a farm just up the road from theirs.

Emily's family farm had a drop dead gorgeous view of the Mountain. One of many unique features of the farm was its water system. Water was pumped from a 10x14x6 wellspring down the hill back up to a third-story cistern to be released by gravity as needed. The neatest feature to me was the water purification system. Emily's brother, Colton, was the family supervisor of this system

which periodically required replacement. He would take his fishing pole down to the well hole, lift the cover and fish for the native trout that had been on duty for several months. By then, the trout was 12 inches long and ready to be a good breakfast, and it was replaced by a trout minnow of 4 to 5 inches as its replacement! Honest, this is not a fish story!

Emily and Jane were in the same grades as Herb and I. I suspect our first interaction as a foursome was likely badminton. Herb and I had noticed the net setup on their south yard next to the driveway to their barn. Herb and I loved the game and played it avidly in Connecticut and at the farm. We both thought we were pretty hot stuff and no one in either town ever beat us. So, a match with girls would easily be a push over, and we had plenty of confidence to risk that first interaction. My recall is that they pretty much cleaned our clocks. This was pretty hard to take for two undefeated football-playing boys. I'm sure we played two out of three and then 3 out of 5 etc., but the results were always the same.....Emily and Jane over the Hallas boys. Thankfully to us, there were no witnesses and traffic was always light on the dirt road.

Of course, as boys will, we decided to switch games to a more manly sport of touch football where we unfairly prevailed sufficiently to recharge our bruised egos. The scores, however, were always quite close and there were always a few disputed plays; that always seemed to be the case with any attempt to take on the sisters. We then moved onto croquet with mixed results, as both teams would win and lose. But we all had great fun and the promise of summer romance was fresh in the clear New Hampshire air.

My recall of our first double date was a square dance down at the Pavilion at the Lake. Herb was old enough to drive and I wasn't, as a 14 or 15 year old. I was somewhat clueless about square dancing; however, both of the girls knew the ropes. The dance hall was on the second floor and they sold soda pop and popcorn from the concession stand facing the beach on the first level. As I recall, you got your hand stamped after paying the 25 or 50 cents. I recall wearing a red checked shirt and Emily wore a full denim square dancer's skirt. I'm sure we were "cute" together. Again, it was great fun.

For the next several summers, Herb and I would look forward to going to the farm on weekends or brief one-week vacations with the family since we knew we had some of our own entertainment. My Mom had a yellow Plymouth convertible in those days, and Herb and I would sail down the tree-lined dirt road to see the sisters. Both girls knew hard work around the farm and in the community. They periodically worked at an ice cream stand near the cement plant and then later at other local spots. Our job was either to go and buy a cone and chat or pick them up after their shift to drive them home. The ride to and from those locations was always marvelous fun, especially in the summer with the top down and the fresh pine air about us as we were riding in the back seat of the convertible....oh my!

Herb and I spent one very special pre-football training camp before the start of his junior year at Yale and my junior year at Loomis. He and I drove up to the farm and spent the entire week preparing for pre-season football. It was the middle of August and my parents stayed home to put out the newspaper. Herb and I would train every day by jogging to the pond, swimming and then jogging back to the farm. We cut the winter woodpile and cleared brush from the upper meadow, all to toughen up for the season that lay before us. The girls heard we were at the farm training and drove up to challenge us to some badminton games and dinner on them back at their farm. Such an offer we couldn't and didn't refuse. We had been working pretty hard and were tired of preparing our own lousy food, likely spaghetti and peanut butter sandwiches with marshmallow (my favorite). When we arrived at their farm, Emily and Jane had prepared a fabulous steak dinner with a fresh garden salad with fresh lemonade! Herb and I thought we had died and gone to heaven.

As we all know, it is very hard to maintain a long distance relationship. The onset of college for me, as well as the distance involved, turned my relationship with Emily from a "crush" to one of a very special friendship. I was 17 or 18 the last time I saw Emily. She left for college way out in the Midwest at the University of Michigan.....we called it (and her) the "Big Em" just to tease her.

The years passed. We both married and had our own families. I would occasionally hear about her great kids and her life in California from neighbors. Her Mom and my mother were great friends. While Louise and I were attending an antique show in another town nearby, I came across a painted plate of Emily's farm when it was a destination boarding house (today we call these B & Bs). The plate had been produced in Germany and I knew she would love it. I got her California address from Priscilla and mailed it off. She was thrilled, as I recall.

The years rolled by into the 1990's and as I have already written, I became smitten with research on our farm and our first settler, Peter Holbrook. In attempting to find where he was buried, we discovered that he moved off the Hill and died in 1805. We found his grave in a cemetery a town away from the farm. We attempted to follow where his offspring lived, and determined that one of them had moved to a farm up the road from us. I discovered that our Peter Holbrook was likely related to the Holbrooks who lived/ran what was once known as the Holbrook farm that had become Emily's family's home. Wow! I thought that was pretty cool since I was familiar somewhat with that farm myself.

A few years went by and I revisited my material on Peter Holbrook, re-read the Town History book, and began to ruminate about the Holbrook name and where it would pop up around the County. I then remembered that Emily had an older brother named Holbrook. I thought maybe he was named after the location/the farm and perhaps a fondness towards the prior owners. I decided to write Emily and ask her about the derivation of her older brother's name. She wrote back in awhile that Holbrook was chosen since her father's mother was a Holbrook! Wow! I thought, "what if Emily was a Holbrook?" I wrote her back and asked if she had any idea about her family tree and mentioned my interest in Peter Holbrook, our first settler. She wrote back and kindly enclosed her family tree. When I looked at the family tree from Emily, the first two names at the top of her father's mother's line were John and Mary, followed by Peter! Earlier in the month, Lewis had determined that Peter Holbrook's parents' names were John and Mary. Bingo! Emily was a direct descent of our Peter Holbrook! I never knew that and neither did Emily. This was a big time discovery for me and another neat lesson in living history.

Then, I suddenly felt a cold sweat when I realized that I had formerly dated a direct descendent of the very house I now lived in. Had I dated a ghost?......Yikes!

Postscript: Emily, who lived on what was once the Holbrook farm, is a direct descendent of Peter and Lydia Holbrook, first settlers of our town who built our house. Lydia's last name was Darling. This had evaded Louise and me since the deeds only refer to her as Lydia and she signed with an X. The history books, however, had a Darling family in it; I believe there was a Stephen Darling who married a Scott and lived near Scott's brook. I suspect this person could have been Lydia's brother; however, I have no proof. One of the Scott children is buried in an old cemetery near our farm. She died at age 9 and is one of the few headstones that can be read.

A FLINTY NEW HAMPSHIRITE

June 11, 1999

This sketch is of a 90-year-old man named Bill. I first met Bill when he was attempting to clarify boundary markers on his emerging thousand+ acre preserve. He appeared in a cloud of dust coming up our dirt road driving a dark green 1946 Jeep full of stakes and chainsaws. He wore a red bandana around his neck like Roy Rogers; however, Bill was protecting himself from the dreaded New Hampshire black flies! He pulled over onto the lawn and I stopped mowing our front lawn. Bill said, "About 100 years ago I used to know a man who lived here named Hallas (my father)." Knowing that I was confronted by a very unique and signature image before me, I said in my most Stanleyesque fashion, "And you must be Bill, I presume!" Thus began a friendship with a most remarkable "Flinty" man. The following is only a brief insight into a man I consider a good friend.

Our first activity involved finding the boundary markers between our farm and land Bill had just acquired (100 acres that was sold by Homestead Woolen Mills, partly owned by someone who became a very special friend of ours by the name of Barbara). The new parcel was the furthest east Bill's "kingdom" had come, and he was not as familiar with the property lines. I knew this parcel like the back of my hand and asked him if he'd seen the cellar hole. He said he had not and that he had been over the property many times hunting for it. He was slightly embarrassed when I led him to it, since he had come within feet of it several times and missed it. Bill never missed much in the woods and he was legendary for his skills.

Over the next several years, Louise and I would go out to dinner with Bill and his wife, Elena, or have dinner at our farm or visit with mutual friends. We also visited him and Elena in Florida. Our gatherings were always great fun, as Bill was a real man's man and full of the devil and a ton of fun. He was a man of wealth, but you'd never know it. He also was a man of enormous generosity, and that he also kept to himself.

This next story about Bill begins on a section of a secluded dirt road in "no man's" land. I used it as a short cut to the dump. The road goes for miles and circles the northern parcels of what I call "Bill's Kingdom." You need 4-wheel drive to get through, but the rewards of natural beauty are very much worth the bumpy drive. As I came to a bend in the road, I noticed a dark green Jeep Wrangler approaching from the other direction. I was delighted to see that it was Bill driving his brand new 1999 modified Jeep Wrangler. Bill had lost some nerve control in his left leg over the winter and decided to adapt his body to the demands of his routine in the woods by acquiring a new automatic transmission Jeep. Apparently, his left leg could not work the pedals as required by manual transmission shifting of his 1946

Jeep. He had a custom winch welded to his new Wrangler and a metal plate soldered underneath, as he was prone to go places most men don't dare. I complimented him on his new Jeep and he looked at it fondly and said with a straight face, "Yes they really have made some improvements." I chuckled about that a number of times, since after all, Jeep had had 53 years to make them for Bill! Bill was checking one of his farm gates in "no man's" land, as some of the locals were circumventing his entrances and causing havoc on some of his landscape. This could have been a scene out of the old West (or in this case the old East)! We chatted a few minutes and agreed that we and the wives should get together for dinner soon. Even though Bill was my neighbor, it would take me over 4 miles of bushwhacking to get to his farm from ours. I know....I've done that bushwhack by foot!

A few weeks later, Louise and I invited them over for an early summer cookout dinner on our screened porch. I wondered that night which direction they would arrive from. If they came from the left, it meant that Elena, Bill's lovely wife, would be driving. If they came from the right, it meant that Bill would be driving and Elena would be shell-shocked upon arrival. I heard the car coming from the right. Sure enough, Bill was driving and Elena was white as they bounced off the dirt road and swung into our front lawn. Bill was driving his second new Jeep, again a dark green Jeep Cherokee Sport. I bet Bill got a better deal by buying two: one for "on road" and the other for "off road."

I couldn't help but notice that Bill looked tired as he slowly swung down out of his new horse. I beamed, and pointed across the street to our new 1999 "Chili Pepper Red" Jeep parked under the spreading maple trees. We both laughed and agreed we had made a good purchase. Neither of us had known the other had done so! Bill, with cane in tow, ambled his 6 foot 2 inch, slim frame up the farmyard grade to the porch. I asked him how he was feeling and he said, "I'm a bit tired, I got up at 3:30 a.m. to go trout fishing with my (60+ year old) fishing buddy, Clint. Yes, we had our limit by 6:30 a.m.," as he handed me a package of wrapped trout that felt like a 16-pound shot put! He went on, "The real problem is that we were out last night till 11 p.m. with company!" I immediately knew that what he needed to revive was a good stiff Scotch. As I asked Elena what she wanted to drink, Bill quizzed me about how many drinks he owed me. Bill is the kind of man who refuses to be indebted to anyone at any time. The fact that he owed me a drink from our last meeting in Florida was bothering him. I wasn't going to let him off the hook, so I was telling him that the tally was up to three Scotches and counting this evening. We both liked scotch. While this banter was going on, I could overhear snatches of a grim conversation between Elena and Louise. Rather than interrupt and bring Bill's attention to a grim story that he was the subject of, I continued to exaggerate his debt to me. Finally, in mock exasperation Bill said "Well, damn it....I'll buy you a whole bottle of scotch and we can finish it together the next time you come over to my place!" At that point I said, "You got a deal" and wandered off to the kitchen to fix drinks.

Upon my return, Bill was regaling Louise and Elena with the day's fishing story. Apparently, the day's limit of trout was 6, and he and Clint had caught 5 when Bill hooked one more and Clint hooked 2 more, as Clint fishes with two lines. The dilemma was that the men had to decide which line/lines needed to be cut so as to not be over limit. Two of the three currently on their lines had to be released. The sun was just coming up, so it was difficult to tell which was the largest. Both Bill and Clint claimed theirs was the largest, of course. Clint dropped the smaller of his two and then deferring to his elder fishing buddy, dropping his second fish. Bill, knowing full well the skill of his partner, assumed Clint was actually correct and then released his trout. So the two great fishermen, needing one more for their limit, actually caught three and then released three, an amusing scene for sure.

The evening was most pleasant as it always was with Bill and Elena. We share the simple pleasure of friendship, conversation, and a love for a pleasant evening in the woods of New Hampshire. I cooked some steak and chicken outside on the reconstructed "Pit" and Louise cooked rice and fresh asparagus inside on the stove. We both laughed over how we felt like jumping jacks that evening....in and out and in and out. Eventually, we all settled for coffee and conversation as the sun slipped behind the white pines over the mountain which Bill owns and enjoys. As the shadows began to fall, we all listened quietly to the sounds of an early summer's eve. Eventually, I heard my favorite owl call and then heard it answered by another owl somewhere in "Bill's Kingdom." I explained the sounds to Bill, as I thought that he could pick them up with his hearing aid. He said it reminded him of one of his favorite hunting stories. Apparently he and his hunting partner would use an owl call to let each other know where they were in the woods, should they get separated. On this particular occasion, Bill continued to give the call and to move towards the answering call from his partner. He moved deeper and deeper into the woods. Eventually he realized that the returned call wasn't his partner but a real owl, and he was many more miles into the woods than he intended that trip!

The evening came to a close and we all parted in good cheer. As they pulled out of the yard, I recall thinking how I hoped that I could still drive a new Jeep to a dinner with friends at age 90 some day! Louise and I marveled at how Bill adapted to the many curve balls that life has thrown him. Later that evening Louise filled me in on the horror story that befell Bill a few weeks earlier (the story that I had partially overheard while getting drinks).

According to Elena, a few weeks back Bill and a friend named Don were doing some chores in the deep woods of "Bill's Kingdom." They were checking it out, driving Bill's new Wrangler. Don stopped for lunch in the woods and Bill continued alone in the Jeep to check a gate near some high ground within the "Kingdom." Time went by and Don assumed that Bill must have returned to his farm for lunch so he headed there. Upon his arrival, he found no Bill and a worried Elena. Don retraced his steps and eventually came upon Bill hobbling along on his cane, bloody from head to toe. As the story was reiterated, Bill got into trouble with his new Jeep on a rather steep slope. He lost control of the Jeep and it ran downhill eventually coming to rest on top of a massive 5 foot high boulder. Bill was bounced out and had a cut on his head needing 25 stitches. He had picked himself up and hobbled one and a half miles down the mountain before he met up with Don! Somehow, they cleaned up the cut, and returned to the Jeep to retrieve it before heading to the hospital. The nasty cut on his forehead was completely healed and he had made no mention of the affair to me earlier that evening.

Now there is a "Flinty New Hampshirite" for you!

Two weeks later Louise and I went over to their house for dinner. Of course, I started in on him and the debt of the bottle of Scotch he owed me. He quietly turned to me and said, "Oh yes, you can find it on the counter where I keep my liquor!" I wandered into the closet and there on the counter was a brand new tiny two-ounce Scotch "chaser" bottle! You had to get up really early to get ahead of Bill!

I could hear him chuckling outside in the kitchen.

Bill and Elena have since passed away, sadly. Bill was a couple months shy of 100 when he died in 2008.

A WOMAN NAMED "BARBARA"

I first saw Barbara in the summer of 1953 when she was riding tall in the saddle on her beautiful Chestnut horse with white markings. My brother Herb and I were playing badminton in the front yard at the farm when she and her three daughters rode elegantly past us on our road. All of them were dressed in tweed riding outfits and the image was one of beauty and grace. This was one of many country scenes which were new to the two flatlander brothers. Little did I realize that 40 years later Barbara would become a dear friend. I recall that my mother, who had a horse in college, was very impressed by the scene in 1953.

Forty years later Louise and I formally met Barbara at a gathering at some friends' farm down the hill from us. When we first met Barbara, she had just returned from driving with a female friend all the way out to Washington State and back. She was then a widow and had maintained her independent and adventuresome spirit which we admired so much. Louise and Barbara hit it off quickly, as both had a deep love of flowers and gardening. I immediately became fond of her because of her knowledge about and shared love of nature and the environment. It seems Barbara, a Radcliffe graduate, had a degree in Biology and a keen knowledge of anything that grew in the area and beyond. And so it wasn't long before she would visit the farm and check out Louise's gardens or we would join Barbara and some of our other New Hampshire friends for a treat of Barbara's gourmet fare.

The singular facet to Barbara which Louise and I most admired was her steady, upbeat, positive, curious nature. She was never negative and was always interesting on many levels. Although Barbara was in her 90's, there was never any age difference, as we shared the same perspective on Life and always enjoyed each other's company.

BILL K.

I have two very distinct first memories of Bill K. The first was as a five-year-old watching the soldiers returning home from World War II. Bill and his brother Spencer were marching into the Center in my hometown in Connecticut, dressed in their Navy whites with rifles at their shoulders. My brother and I were in awe as these two handsome young men marched by us. Little did we know we would refer to them as members of "The Greatest Generation" when we were much older. I suspect I was mightily impressed since they were brothers marching together and Herb and I could identify with that fact.

The second memory is clear but less precise. Bill ran the appliance store in my hometown, and was a key advertiser in our family newspaper business. His store carried all the latest emerging electric devices, paints, and lawn equipment galore. However, he did not tolerate any childish behavior in his establishment. In short, he ran a tight ship – unlike the hardware store in town where a kid could get away with almost anything, as the owner of that store was nearly blind as a bat as we used to say. He had coke bottle glasses and could barely see over the counter. I seldom went into Bill's store and never explored the aisles as I did in the hardware store.

Bill and his beautiful wife were friends of my Mom and Dad. In fact, I consider them responsible for introducing us to our farm in New Hampshire as I wrote about earlier. Bill loved the outdoors and was an avid fisherman and hunter. Later, he became hooked on making his farm a prize-winning one, and he even gleaned an award for top farm in the County.....not bad for a flatlander! Bill loved to trout fish, as did my Dad. Each had their own favorite pools and sections of the same brook that wandered down from our higher ground to lower ground to the east of Bill's farm. I recall my Dad being annoyed that Bill continued to out-fish him. Dad would catch 5 keepers and Bill would have 10 keepers. Dad tried to uncover where Bill bagged them, and began to work his way towards the area. Bill had a section of the lower brook where he had found good access to some beaver dams, and he wouldn't divulge where the access was. Dad and I got close one time, but somehow we'd always end up scaring the trout and would come home empty-handed.

Bill's other fabled skill was horseshoes. I am not sure where he developed the skill, but he was legendary in the area as well as in Connecticut. I never knew anyone who could beat him. He had a "pit" parallel to the dirt road and stone walls of his New Hampshire farm. Any time around dusk, we would see him pitching shoes when we drove by. You could always tell when he was pitching, as it would be accompanied by the sound of the clang of the metal hitting the stake, usually a ringer! My brother eventually gained enough confidence and skill to challenge Bill; however, he faced the same consequences as the rest of the mere mortals did. Bill was a "natural" horseshoe pitcher.

As I wrote earlier, I was always apprehensive of Bill K. and his disciplinarian ways. As I grew older, I became aware that this was not really a true picture of the man. And as I grew even older, he seemed to grow into a warm, approachable man. Somewhere along the line, we met and developed a close relationship. I discovered that he had the same devilish behavior that I can be accused of. He and I would talk by phone most every Friday night after we would arrive at the farm. We would chat for hours. I discovered that he and I had a lot in common with interests as well as shared experiences growing up. We were separated by roughly twenty years; however, we had done the same things as kids growing up in our town in Connecticut. This sharing of childhood experiences was a cherished part of my relationship with Bill that evolved later in his life.

The two "Bills" that I have just portrayed had a close relationship and were a real hoot to be around. The two of them would be an Abbott and Costello act whenever they were together. I would laugh so hard it would bring tears to my eyes. The two men shared a love of the outdoors, cooking with wood stoves or over an outdoor fire. Both had a passion for the "GI" Jeep from the 40's and tried to outlast each other's Jeep. Each would try to outdo the other endlessly.

Bill K. and I also shared an interest in log cabins! Bill owned a mountaintop behind his farm to the west,

100

deeper in the woods. He cut a jeep trail to it and eventually built a log cabin on top with a magnificent view. He helped inspire me to build my log cabin down by our brook. I guess in some ways the two Bills and I were what I'd call "throwbacks," as we admired many of the old outdoor ways of doing things.

GERRY M.

No chapter on "Special People" from the farm era would be complete without including our beloved neighbor, Gerry. The real man was not what you saw with a first impression. Gerry had bluster and an image which was a mask. He had a heart of gold and lived by the golden rule and more. Few knew he was a veteran of three theaters of operation in World War II, and he was an eagle scout in his youth.

He and his lovely wife and family moved to New Hampshire in the early 1960's. It seemed Gerry wanted to get back to nature and real people instead of what he referred to as the "phoniness" of Fairfield County, Connecticut where he had pursued a plumbing career after the War. Our small town was a great choice for him. I must admit my parents were not sure whether he'd make it through the first winters which are rough on our Hill. He did, however, make it through many winters, and Gerry settled into the place he dearly loved and always wanted.......a little piece of God's green acre.

Gerry's ethic was simply to "love thy neighbor." He helped hundreds of folks in town over the years. I was truly impressed, at his memorial service which Louise and I attended, by how many people spoke of his aid over the years. I am especially indebted to him, as my widowed mother was one of the many. Gerry always kept an eye on her and the farm for us and helped her whenever needed. My mother would not have enjoyed her last years at the farm if it were not for his kindness.

I got to know him better in those days. Whenever he would drive by in his Jeep, he would stop and come up to the porch to chat a bit and maybe have a beer. He would always have something to say about most things, and sometimes it was outrageous, but likely true. His language was always salty, and my daughters would claim to have learned most of their swear words from him through their bedroom doors after I'd sent them packing. Gerry had earned and exercised his freedom of speech and choice of life style especially with his service to the country. I recall him telling me he was at "D-Day" as a Tug Boat Captain, pulling concrete blocks (Mulberry harbours) from England to France to set up the dock structures to advance the liberation of Europe. Like many of his generation, he rarely talked about it, but he wasn't to be intimidated by anyone on most any subject. He was a kind and generous family man and he and Eleanor raised a great family, many of whom would help my aging and ailing parents. Louise was also very fond of Gerry, and she was one of the fortunate ones who got to know the interesting and kind man that he was.

Our town did not have a full-time police department, so if anything ever happened up on our dirt road, it was usually Gerry who kept the peace. He would run off an errant vagrant or misplaced hunter or trash-throwing visitor. We all felt a little safer when Gerry was around. He could smell trouble and nip it in the bud and then have a Bud.

Gerry has a grave marker in an old cemetery behind his farm where the Scott girl is buried (which I wrote about earlier). The location is a perfect place for a kind and gentle big man.

ALLEN H. A/K/A AL PARKER A/K/A "SMOKEY"

Allen is related to our first settler, Peter Holbrook, and lives in the most attractive historic house in town, if not the entire county. As a boy, he spent all his summers at this farm and graduated from the "hard knocks" summer camp in town.

It was during these summers that Allen developed a love of and skill in baseball. He played for the camp and loved to see his team beat the larger camp in town. He played for various area recreation teams and became a "Cracker Jack" shortstop. He went on to play varsity baseball in college and earned the nickname of "Smokey." During his upperclassman years there he played semi-pro ball. This move put his college playing at risk, so he played under an assumed name of "Al Parker."

His love of sports continues in retirement with his support of New England's favorite teams: the Red Sox, Celtics, Patriots, and Bruins. He has also converted one of the rooms at his farm into a "Sports Bar" theme of great renown. Allen also has a love of golf, and he had a history of playing it extremely well.

"HOLIDAY MEL"

Columbus Day Weekend 1995

I was hiking in the Adirondacks with Cody, our Golden Retriever, when Louise first met Mel. She was driving up to the farm with our newly rescued "Molly", a cute little 5-month-old Bichon, and "Max", our elder statesman Bichon. Apparently, Molly was a tad stressed and had upchucked a few times in the car on the way north. Louise turned onto the dirt road and wound her way up the hill. As she approached the power line clearing, there he was.....an enormous Bull Moose, the size of a large working horse with a six-foot rack to boot! Louise immediately named him Mel as she introduced herself, I am told. Of course, yours truly was likely lost again in the Adirondacks.

Memorial Day 1996

It was a gloriously sunny and warm Memorial Day. I decided to open the "Pit" and cook some "Hank Hallas Burgers" outside. This was the inaugural christening of the "Pit." As I recall I even used some dead apple wood to help flavor the burgers and create some nice wood smoke. I delivered the platter to our outdoor glass table and iron chairs and we sat down to have a taste. As I took my first bite, I noticed a huge

Moose entering the top of the meadow where the deer usually enter. Mel had come to lunch - or so he thought! The dogs were lounging around outside and Louise's immediate thought was for their safety, as they would pick up Mel's scent and run up to him. I stood up and attempted to head for the dogs to help collar them. Unfortunately for me, my belt loop got tangled in the back of the chair, so I was moving with a chair appendage as I tried to get the dogs. The commotion was just too much for Mel; he wheeled and fled the scene, much to our disappointment and amazement.

4th of July 1997

Another bright and glorious Fourth of July weekend started with a picture perfect summer Saturday morning. I gathered the "boys" (Max and Cody) and left the girls (Louise and Molly) to "luxuriate" (which was Louise's term for reading with a first cup of coffee) and headed to the cabin for my Saturday morning coffee. We settled in on the cabin porch; me in a rocker with a coffee mug and the boys by my side. Max jumped up into my lap as usual and we began to read the morning mail. That ritual entails my eyesight and their noses checking for any critters moving about. All was quiet except for the bugs and the birds humming around and over the beaver pond. It was a lush and lovely sight!

I had just finished my coffee and set the mug down when I thought I heard a sound off to the right, near the beaver dam out of sight. Sure enough, I heard it again. It sounded like the splash of a beaver tail in the water. Oh good, I thought, maybe we would get a daytime sighting of one of the beavers that live there. That would be a somewhat rare sight, as beavers are usually nocturnal. I strained to hear the splash again, and then I heard a splash, splash, splash, splash. This sound had a rhythm to it that didn't match any beaver that I had heard before.....what the hell was it? My first thought was that it was likely a deer drinking there and deciding to wander along the bank....that's cool, I thought.

My next move was to collar the hounds....first Max in my lap and then Cody. I cuffed both their collars so they wouldn't bolt or bark. I then leaned forward in my rocker to see if I could ID the creature, as I suspected it might be moving towards us. From prior experience, I had learned that animals who walk into your zone/area act more natural than when you walk into their zone/area. First, they are less likely to pick up your scent if you are upwind and secondly, there is no startle factor from sound or smell. So the three of us essentially froze in place and waited for the entrance. The area of the dam is blocked by a graceful Evergreen which provides visual cover for any animals arriving around the dam.

The sound of the splash, splash, splash, splash became louder and the cadence confirmed a four-legged critter. Then, the dark blackish-brown body made its appearance as it cleared the limbs, and suddenly the six-foot-wide rack of Mel shown brightly in the sunlight of the beaver pond. Mel in all his 2,500-pound glory made his entry splash, splash, splash, splash. He continued until he was directly in front of us - about 50 feet smack dab dead center. The three of us had our jaws lying on the floor of the cabin porch. We were all too stunned to do anything but stare! Mel stopped and took a chew and wiggled his head a tad. At that movement, Cody barked dead air as I practically had choked him silent; same for Max. Both peed in their empty pants!

I was in semi-shock! I thought, "I can't move or let the dogs go, but I'd really like to take them inside the cabin so they won't get hurt." What was Mel going to do when he finally saw us? And then Mel did turn and look me square in the eye.....my Kodak moment! Many thoughts raced through my mind and then a light bulb went off. Louise usually talks to wild animals, especially while gardening. She had had a great time talking face-to-face with Tess (our resident Tree swallow) just the other day. I thought, "Why not? What harm could it do?" So in my calmest, most natural voice, I said, "Hi Mel! Happy Fourth of July........How's the family?" (Honest.) And then I waited for his reply. He swallowed, chewed again and shook a fly off his mane, and then looked to the far bank. So I continued, "Well Mel, it certainly is a nice sunny day.....don't you think?" He wiggled a bit and then lifted his left hoof up about half way and then stomped it down in the mud and then looked across the pond again.

I really thought by then that maybe he was trying to say or tell me something. But what was on his mind, I thought. What or where was he trying to go? Then it occurred to me that the line of departure, should he leave our presence, would force him into the deeper part of the pond where the original brook bed is located, and that would come up to his chest and would be a tad chilly. Maybe, just maybe, he didn't want to cross the pond there, but he really wanted to come towards the cabin and use my footpath about 25 feet to my left. And so I decided to go with that logic and said, "Mel, that's alright....you don't have to cross the deep part. You can use my footpath over there!" And I motioned in that direction with my head, nodding to the left. Max and Cody wiggled like crazy. They thought I was nuts talking to Mel.

Mel nodded his head after I spoke and motioned. He marched towards us on an angle heading for the footpath. He came within 25 feet of us and ambled out of the pond edge and trotted down my footpath out of sight. And now I am a true believer in talking to the animals!

When I got back to the house, Louise christened him "Holiday Mel," as he seemed to always make his appearance on holidays!

Labor Day Weekend 1997

We arrived at the farm in the dark on a clear Friday night. I pulled the car up to the porch and its lights shown up the meadow. I was excited to see how my sunflowers were doing at the top of the vegetable garden. I had a row of 16 sunflowers which stood about 10 feet tall and had a seed pod the size of a steering wheel, bent over with its weight. I had been admiring them for a few weeks and hoped for a good show this Labor Day weekend. I was puzzled as I peered in dark shadows of the car's lights up the meadow. It seemed that I didn't have all 16 sunflowers, but I wasn't really sure.

The next morning I walked into the back yard and peeked at my crop. Oh my! I could only count 8 sunflower seed heads out of the 16 stalks! What a curiosity, it seemed! Where did the other 8 seed heads go? As I walked up to the garden for a closer inspection, I thought maybe a squirrel had begun to harvest them, or maybe a deer had nibbled them. As I did a closer inspection, I was stunned not to see any debris. The ground around the garden was clean as could be. The heads had been nipped off and 8 still hung in their glory. What a puzzle! Louise joined me and we discussed what had befallen our garden sunflower crop. I figured there had to be some evidence somewhere. So, I began my forensic study. I decided to look in the garden itself....no crumbs, no scrap; however, there were some tell tale footprints.....Holiday Mel's footprints! He must have eaten the whole thing – all 8 and left us 8!

What a guy!

Halloween Weekend 2003

It was a stormy Friday night on Halloween – spooky, dark, and windy, as we made our way onto our road, heading for the farm. When we were about a mile from the farm, we spotted a large critter ambling out of the side road onto the road in front of us. It was Holiday

Mel! And he wasn't happy. I slowed down so as not to scare or hurt him (or us). However, we were both taking the same dirt road towards the farm about a mile away. I slowed down to a total crawl and he continued to amble along right in front of us. I thought he would cross the road and split into the woods, but no, not "Holiday Mel." He continued to walk slowly in front of us the whole way. Every now and then he would turn and give us his ugliest look as if to say "What, are you guys still there? Get lost!" He clearly was not happy with the weather or his trackers. He led us all the way to the farm where we turned in and he continued on down the road. The next morning I found his hoof tracks around the Jeep where he had doubled back to smell us out!

4

✿ ✿ ✿

Cabin Tales

CABIN FEVER

The best I can recall, I caught Cabin Fever in the early 1980's. I had spent many wonderful men's weekends camping and hiking in the Adirondacks. Those adventures are captured in a document called "Men's Weekend, an Adirondack Journal." Several of these hikes included a destination lunch to an Adirondack "lean-to." The simple and functional design really captured my imagination for wilderness trekking. They provide useful shelter from the elements and warmth once one masters the skill of building a fire near the opening so that the smoke goes up but the warm air rolls in.

Additionally, whenever we hiked up to my friend's cabin on 11th Mountain, we passed a deserted but magnificent log cabin which was built in the 1800's. It was a classic. I made a sketch of it and then measured its dimensions from head to foot as a model for a future effort. The cabin was just too perfect to pass up. At the time I knew it was probably beyond my skill and time availability, but I wanted some plans. It occurred to me that maybe the simple "lean-to" was within my reach. I decided to measure and count the number of logs in the typical classic Adirondack lean-to as well. The number of logs was 41, each about 12 feet long and one foot in

diameter. After a bit of rumination it occurred to me that if I cut just one white pine log on a weekend trip to the farm I would have the building materials within one calendar year. Now that seemed doable, so I began to cut and skin one white pine a weekend. The tree had to be straight, cut by ax, limbed, and skinned.

The interesting thing about this approach is that it gave me one year to decide where to locate the lean-to. And so I spent the next four seasons testing various sites around the property which would fulfill the promise of a good choice. I felt that a good choice must meet the following objectives:

a. have a pleasant protected view of natural beauty;

b. allow me to see animals without spooking them, a blind;

c. provide shelter from excessive cold wind or southern summer heat;

d. separate from the farm but not excessively distant either.

I came up with four spots: the upper edge of the meadow above the farm; near a bend in the brook which my mother loved; the northeast corner of the property near the "rocketty rock;" and amidst the pines near the beaver pond near the western border of our land. Each season I would make a visit to the sites, check the wind, the sunlight, the view, and any animal sign. Each season yielded different results and one clear winner in my not-so-humble opinion....the beaver pond. Each of the other sites scored well for one or two seasons, but the beaver dam scored on all four seasons. So now I had my lean to site and mounting pile of white pine logs which were curing on dry ground.

In the summer of 1985 daughter Liz and I took a tent camping trip around the Rockies. One of our stops included Cody, Wyoming where we deviated from our plan and camped in a "Cozy Cabin" in the local K.O.A. campground outside of town. This little cabin was a sweetheart, complete with indoor bunk beds, a window, and a tiny front porch. I counted the logs required to build it and came up with 46. And so, I decided to modify my Adirondack lean-to to be a cabin. It was actually a lean-to with a closed front wall with a window and a door as well as a few feet reserved for a porch. That became the basis of my beaver pond cabin design. Now all I had to do was build it!

Upon return, I continued to finish up gathering the logs, skinning, and limbing. Around this time, my Adirondack hiking friend visited me at the farm. I took him down to show him the site. He said, "Are you going to use a 12 or 16 stone foundation?" I looked at him cross-eyed....."What's a 12 or 16 stone foundation?" I said. He then proceeded to describe it and then started to roll stones into place upon which all the foundation logs would rest nice and level, and square and off the ground to prevent rot! It took about an hour and I was ready to start laying the cross beams to lay the floor! He had had prior construction experience and helped talk me through the beginning steps. His son had already also caught the same "cabin fever" and was building his own lean-to on the brow of 11th Mountain.

After placing the beams and then nailing a floor down I began to erect the side walls using my year-old log pile. By this time, the logs had cured and their weight was considerably less. I rolled them into place and began to notch the butt ends for the corners. I'd never done this before and my skill level was not the best. I told myself this cabin was practice for a real one up in the Adirondacks when I retired. About this time in my life, the spring of 1988, I had met Louise and she fell in love with New Hampshire. It reminded her of her summers in the North Carolina Mountains from her childhood. She too became smitten by the log cabin effort and wanted to help. I wasn't quite sure what tasks would fit her skills, but she was game, and she became a pretty good log-skinner and chinker. I was able to get the walls about 5-

feet high all the way around and then it started to get a bit hairy. The higher I went, the trickier it got to lift a twelve-foot by one-foot diameter log above my head to swing it into a poorly cut notch! The roof support task is a whole separate and dangerous story.

I had decided that the roof needed to be supported by two sturdy logs which would carry the weight of the roof and not fail due to pine rot in the years to come. I had also determined that some red oak trees growing across the brook south of the site by about 150 yards would be perfect. I dropped them and cut four members to 10-foot lengths. I did this without any clue as to how I would move these heavyweights to my building site. There were no roads, paths or any manners to get to them other than bushwhack! I decided that something would occur to me and that they were the perfect choice to hold up the roof and the front porch!

About a month after I had cut the red oak beams, we had a devil of a rainstorm. The ponds and brooks were over their banks and the whole countryside seemed to be awash. I suddenly had a brain storm that, just perhaps, my red oak logs could float, and if so, maybe, just maybe we could float the four of them down the brook to a spot fairly close to the log cabin site. I wasn't sure they would float since they were heavy as sin, but I didn't have any other idea about how to move them! So I bushwhacked to the site and began to roll the four logs to the bank of the brook and ease them in....and yes, they did float! I then waded into the brook and eased them down stream about 100 yards with Louise's help to guide

120

the logs away from hitting the banks. This was tricky, as I had to slide them up and over a few smallish beaver dams. The logs were pushed out of the brook but still needed to be slid about 40 yards to the site. Louise was game to help, so I tied a rope around the butt end and we began to drag them along a footpath to the site. This was onerous work and probably accounts for Louise's back issues. But the logs were finally at the site. Done!

Now the trick was to stand each of the four of them up and maneuver them into place to hold both the front porch rafters and the roof center beam (an 8x8 fir beam). I hoisted the first red oak beam up and turned to fetch my hammer to nail down a holding board. When I turned, the beam tilted and fell off the porch, missing Louise by 2 feet.......a real disaster had been just inches away! Thank God it missed her, as she had just gotten off the porch and below the fall line.

As I had reached the 6-foot level, I knew I needed some additional help with the porch rafters and such. My daughter Liz (the soon to be budding architect) was really into it. She and her friend, Erik, spent one entire weekend helping me frame the top of the interior walls, porch rafters, and roof supports. Then, all that remained was to acquire and nail down a metal roof. I decided to select a metal roof because of its durability and because the key to longevity in New Hampshire is always a good roof!

The rest of the construction was kept simple and fun. I recycled some old storm windows for light from above. I nailed together a framed door, then I used a chain saw to cut out a front window and constructed a hinged shutter. Louise's small hands were excellent in "chinking" the logs with our homemade mortar. The overall effect was quite professional and finished.

I really wanted to have a stove for the cabin. I had an old Morso stove from my Connecticut days; however, that stove was not good at providing quick heat. I found the solution at an auction one late winter Saturday night. I bid $25 for a neat Franklin stove. The only problem once again was how to get the 250-pound stove to the cabin site in the dead of winter. Well, as I ruminated that snow (frozen water) can be your friend, I decided that I could slip the stove onto a toboggan and pull it down to the cabin on top of the snow. Once at the porch, I built a snow ramp so I could pull the toboggan up onto the porch and deplane the stove on the front porch for the winter! Done!

I also wanted a fireplace outside in front of the short porch for summer cooking and entertainment. The key issue to that was how to get a large stone "fireback" for the stone fireplace. The fireplace was simple enough but the "fireback" stone presented a unique problem and solution. The following summer I invited a young man from work named Pete up to the farm. I needed his strong back to assist in acquiring a massive stone from the nearby stone wall over to the fireplace site. It seemed simple enough and I thought the two of us were strong enough to roll the flat side monster to its spot.......wrong! It turned out that the stone weighed about 300 to 400 pounds and didn't want to be tumbled anywhere. What to do? I sat on the porch, lit a cigar, and thought awhile. What would the Romans have done? What would the Egyptians have done? Why sure....they would have rolled it into place on rollers. So, I cut two dozen red maple saplings about three inches in diameter and one foot long. I laid them onto a footpath as a road and then we rolled the beast stone for the 30 yards. That stone is forever to be known as "La Roc." Done!

The other finishing details included trimming the underbrush around the cabin to unleash only wild blueberry bushes and to install the fireplace. My friend, John, assisted on the installation of the Franklin fireplace and was present to light the first match. When the smoke came out of the chimney, I yelled, "We have a new Pope!"

Done!

TOP SECRETS TO GREAT SIGHTINGS

When I was a youngster, I read stories about famous Indian scouts and hunters who appeared to have the knack for sneaking up on any kind of critter in the wild. I remember imitating their secret moves as I moved about in the woods surrounding the farm. First, I would walk quietly and be sure not to break any twigs......that usually meant I had to look at the ground constantly, which was its own skill. But how could I see any critters if my head was down? And if my head was up to look around, how could I not step on the twigs? That was one of life's great puzzles for a 10 year old. And of course I couldn't talk or whistle or throw things or cock my .22 rifle or I would scare the critters for sure. I practiced being a good Indian scout for years and occasionally I'd be rewarded with a good critter sighting. Most of the time I shot blanks for my efforts.

As I got older, I continued the routine as I moved in the woods, but it wasn't until I spent time at the cabin building, resting, and observing that I began to uncover the Top Secrets to good critter viewing! It was a gradual process and I didn't realize it until I had finished my apprenticeship. Here's what I learned using 20-20 hindsight (pun intended).

General Rules of Viewing Engagement

1. Indian scouting moves are good; you need to be quiet and move quietly in the woods.

2. When you move in the woods, move slowly and stop frequently.

3. Look for movement in the woods around you. Spotting movement against a still background is the number one skill and key to good observation experiences.

4. Look for outlines that do not match expectations. This is the second most important skill. What shape in your field of vision doesn't match your expectation or your memory of "place" from prior visits? This skill has served me very well at the cabin where I have visual memory of almost every tree, bush and boulder....color, shape, and location. If something doesn't match or fit, it likely is an animal, frozen, waiting to flee.

5. Know the direction of the wind. If you are down-wind, the animal may not smell your presence, and if you are up-wind, it will likely smell your presence. So good animal sighting is not just about the sound you make in the woods, smell counts and movement counts.

6. When you physically move into a wild animal's territory, expect any wild animal to "flee or fight." These moments are unexpectedly fast when they happen. When

you scare a bear, deer or a moose it will bolt instantaneously and the sighting opportunity is limited.

Top Secret Rules when Animals Move into Your Field of Vision

1. When a wild animal moves into your territory (i.e. cabin porch viewing) then it is a whole new ballgame. There is a whole new subset of rules that come into play, many of which I am still learning:

a. The animal moving in is less likely to be fearful;

b. The animal is more likely to respect you and your right to the "place";

c. It is possible that the animal will exhibit curiosity about you. I had a Pileated Woodpecker completely check me out after I had hung a new bird box. I have also had fawns walk up to the cabin within yards to see me for themselves;

d. You still need to be careful about any sound or quick movement, but both will be tolerated to a limit (see the Tale on "Holiday Mel.");

e. You will be allowed to talk to the animal and the animal may or may not respond. The talking can be of the human variety as well as animal imitation, i.e. deer snorting, owl calls;

f. Your scent is likely to be more tolerated because you are not the visitor; the animal is;

g. The visiting animal is less likely to know or see that you are there....this is the reverse of when you move into their territory;

h. There seems to be a physical distance away that becomes tolerated for mutual movement without flight. This seems to apply to both birds and animals;

i. Beavers seem to have their own sense of territory and will chase you off their beaver dam (when you are fishing, for example) by slapping their tails and diving in front of you. That usually works since the trout aren't going to be biting after one of those explosive tail slaps!

2. Patience is key in solitary viewing. I developed a set of rules of thumb as follows:

a. When it is time to leave, wait five more minutes;

b. When the first 5 minutes is up, repeat waiting another five minutes;

c. When the second 5 minutes is up, wait a third five minutes. I have found (after trial and error) great viewing success within the second or third wait. I developed this after standing up prior to the first 5 minutes and scaring many animals who were just about to enter my field of vision. This method has solved that problem and given me considerably enhanced viewing enjoyment.

If you are willing to try these tips, you too may be rewarded!

CABIN TALE FROM NEW HAMPSHIRE

June 4, 2001

Introduction:

This short tale is being sent to those of you who have visited or are familiar with our little log cabin in New Hampshire:

Context:

This last year (2000) had been a difficult one for the two Wood Duck boxes which I mounted near/in the beaver pond to attract nesting Wood Ducks. First, the box on the far side of the pond was trashed when a granddaddy beaver chewed down a mighty 75-foot tall red oak which fell into the pond, crushing a smaller tree from which I had hung the box. The box lay in water 30 feet out until late fall. I finally retrieved it on a cold November day and set it in the sun to dry out, then remounted it on a new tree and added some pine chips inside for new nesters. I froze my "tuckus" and smashed my fingers nailing it back up. But I hoped for better days in the spring of 2001. The second box, closer to the cabin, was mounted on a dead pine tree for 7 or 8 successful years. However, the dead pine succumbed to rot and had fallen over in December of 2000. Again I waded out on thin ice, remounted it on a post which I propped up in the mud after cutting a hole in the ice. And again I hoped for a better day in the spring of 2001. I came very close to chalking up the far box to a natural disaster and applying to "FEMA" for relief!

Dateline June, 2001, 7:00 a.m. Log Cabin Porch

It's raining again as Cody, Max (the two male dogs) and I sit on the porch of the cabin while I drink my morning coffee and await Nature's visitors of the day! I am not optimistic that the black flies and mosquitoes have decided to sleep in because the rain is heavy. During prior weekends, I have had several sightings, some noteworthy.....the best was a "Hooded Merganser" (Duck) who dropped into the pond in front of me and after preening himself, decided to take a nap! This is one of the most handsome birds in the world, second only to the male Wood Duck, in my not-so-humble opinion. I also had a Great Blue Heron drop in with his 7-foot wide wing span, along with my current favorites "Larry, Curly and Moe"....three male Mallards who spend most of the time with their butts up in the air as they feed off the bottom of the shallow beaver pond....hence my nickname for them. They hang around and move together and seem to chat quite a bit about the weather, the stock market, and the Red Sox.

Cody curls up on the floor next to my chair, Max jumps up into my lap and I settle in with my commuter mug of coffee. I scan the horizon for any movement; nothing is moving. I look to my extreme right over my shoulder and spot 6 pink "Lady Slippers" (wild orchids) standing tall close to the stone wall……..now that's a great image, I reflect. Occasionally the pups will lift their heads, and their noses will twitch as they read the morning mail of visitors nearby in the area as yet unseen. I have found that my eyesight is better than theirs, but their noses are far better than mine and we seem to be in a tie for our hearing. The rain continues to fall. A Red Winged Blackbird begins to sing and flit from one side of the pond to the other. Eventually he decides to perch on a floating log in the middle of the pond. This is the first year I recall Red Winged Blackbirds using this beaver pond. Then, very quickly and quietly, as soft as a knife through butter, a small duck slips into the pond and appears in front of me in the misty pond. I am startled, but not totally surprised, because that is how most natural visitors usually arrive…….suddenly, quietly and then as John Madden says, "Boom" there it is! As I strain to identify my new visitor, it dawns on me that she (not highly colored) is most probably the female companion to the Hooded Merganser; so this is a real thrill. She is extremely agile and athletic as she scoots and bobs about.

Eventually she heads for the log in the middle of the pond where the Red Winged Blackbird is perched. She aggressively scoots after him and snaps at him to make him move, which he immediately does! Mr. Blackbird wasn't going to mess with Ms. Merganser! And just as suddenly, Larry, Curly and Moe crash into the pond....the three idiot Mallards. These male clowns flopping into the pond were about as graceless as their

Hollywood namesakes. The wake from their landing threw additional logs and debris up onto the shore and the Blue Jays nearby gave a Tsunami alert cry! Meanwhile, Ms. Merganser quickly and quietly preened herself on the log and then slipped gently back into the water. I was a happy camper, as I had not expected to see anything this wet morning. As I was counting my blessings, Ms. Merganser lifted off the water in a quick and very graceful low flight path. My immediate thought was, "Shucks! The show is over for today.....only the cartoon characters of Larry, Curly and Moe remain for my viewing pleasure!" Suddenly Ms. Merganser turns to the right, still flying about 2 to 3 feet off the water and heads directly for the Wood Duck box on the far side of the pond, and WHAM!....she hits the hole and disappears inside. She's nesting in the far Wood Duck box!....the very one I almost gave up on! I sit back with the rest of my coffee and listen to Cody and Max yawn and snore. Meanwhile, the three butts continue to bob in the middle of the pond and the rain continues to fall.

TALES FROM A NEW HAMPSHIRE CABIN

Some of you have visited the cabin from which I write and to which I often refer. For those of you who haven't been there, it is a simple log cabin on a trout brook and beaver dam in a quiet corner of our New Hampshire property. I visit often on weekends and make little and big discoveries.....mostly little ones, that I like to share.

Palm Sunday 2002

Louise and I decided to get a jump on "opening up" this year with the mild winter. So, we spent Palm Sunday weekend making beds, unpacking stuff, setting out stuff, reconnecting the water, praying that the furnace will come on etc. Most of you have a little experience in those fun routines which must be accomplished before the "settling in" takes place. We still have 6 inches of new snow, but the weather was mild, overcast, and dreary. I suppose if one thinks about it, Palm Sunday might be a tad dreary considering the news of the Christian Story that bears its name. It has always been a significant day of the year for me, as my mother always tried to make it to her church that Sunday. My brother and I usually accompanied her. I discovered that the tradition most probably dated back in our family to the same date that the Civil War ended, and that date was a huge emotional time for our country. So I suspect the event became ingrained as family traditions do without knowing the "Why?" generations later.

My visit to the cabin sans dogs (they stayed in Connecticut with my stepson Mike) was deeply quiet. No sounds, no birds, no animal tracks in the snow, only some ice on the pond. It was as if the dreary day made for a dreary place in nature. That seems to happen oftentimes. The only thing moving was a small grayish bird we suspect is a Kinglet who flitted from spot to spot and made no sound. Somber was the mood and the only hope of spring and its glory days was in my mind's eye.

Following Weekend: Easter Sunday 2002

What a difference a week makes! Louise and I returned to the farm with the dogs, with pleasant weather galore, and it was as if the earth had been moved in our little corner of the world. As I made my way to the cabin for my coffee, the snow underfoot had shrunk to 2-3 inches deep. However, new signs of life had appeared....a fawn print with her mother, a small bear print, a large coyote print, squirrel tracks and some very funny looking turkey tracks......(and I wasn't following myself as Louise might suggest). As I approached the cabin, I was reminded of the great "Overture" from *Porgy and Bess*....one of my all-time favorites as the market square awakens in New Orleans. Well, I had the equivalent in nature....the Pileated Woodpecker was hammering his raucous tune; the Canadian Geese were trumpeting; the Robins and Blue Jays were going at it....it was a real street scene at nature's market down by the cabin!

The pond at the cabin seemed still at first, without any movement. Then, a small pair of one-year-old Wood Ducks paddled around way over by the bulrushes. Shortly thereafter, I saw a "snowball" of white on the water as a Hooded Merganser flushed his comb and glanced my way. It seemed he was particularly still and guardian-like....and then it dawned on me that he was on duty and Ms. Merganser was in the wood duck box checking out this year's rental site! A few minutes later, out came her head and then, Splash! Down she came from the box to join the Mr. and paddle off....a nice early morning sighting.

I hustled back to the farmhouse with the news of Easter morn and then we headed to St. James Episcopal Easter 8 a.m. service. It was a glorious day and the service was most pleasant. The rector spoke of faith and the awe of Christ's coming, the Resurrection, and such things. He described a favorite Christian female poet....I believe her name is Morris or Norris....who teaches elementary school in the Dakota's. He spoke of the unfettered awe of children as they have the openness to see and accept items of faith which we adults are quick to dismiss. His point of the awe of children and his message of faith stuck with me the rest of the day and beyond. On the way back to the farm, the beauty of the day hung everywhere. As we drove down the dirt road towards the brook below our farmhouse, I spotted a black flash near a stone wall. Most of the snow was gone by then and the green things of Nature weren't green yet. It looked like a black weasel....I slowed down.....MINK! Yes! It was a black-tailed mink with a jet black body. Both Louise and I got a good look. The last time I saw a mink at the farm was when I was 10 years old....and I was filled with awe.

What a difference from Palm Sunday to Easter Sunday.

I guess I am a believer!

THE LAST SWIM OF SUMMER

Dateline: September 8, 2003

Every year since I can remember I have had a swimming ritual which is two-fold.....What will be the first day at the start of the summer that I first swim in the Pond? Which day will be the last swim? Both dates are perilous to predict. Is it a cool or early warm spring or is it a cool or humid early fall? I never know. I merely look back some cold bleak day (usually in November) as I pass the Pond and think "yes, I don't think I'll be swimming in this Pond again till next spring!"

I am in the midst of the second annual ritual as I write this.....when does swimming end in 2003? Warm, bright, sunny days in September bode well for the lingering glory of a refreshing dip. Usually the end date is pre-occasioned by a late fall lawn mow or the splitting of the winter wood pile......(which was partially the case yesterday). The day was clear, bright, and sunny, and the water was cool and delightful. As I put my toes in the water I couldn't help but notice......no noise from the Camp; no one sailing on the pond, and nobody at the house to my right.....just yours truly. I indeed had the entire pond to myself, quite rare this year!

To be sure, I was indeed alone, I scanned the shoreline a full 360 degrees. As I looked at the edge of the beach, I spotted a few salamanders, a few small bass, and a tiny school of minnows. So, I was all by myself except for Nature's creatures who really own the place. As I mused on this again, it occurred to me that I was probably the interloper, visitor, flatlander "extraordinaire." So be it....I dove in and felt the comfortable rush of cold water on a warm brow. I bobbed to the surface and resumed my shoreline scan of the liquid horizon to double check my minority position.

And then, as is so often the case in nature, if you really concentrate, forms and images can be spotted....usually of three persuasions....the first is that of movement....something moves and your eyes pick it up; the second is form....something you see doesn't fit the natural, normal place of things....and the third one is of sound....a sound stirs your sensory attention. I heard a sound across the pond....I thought it was a fish jumping....highly likely but I couldn't spot it. I knew something was there, so I resumed my 360-degree liquid scan for the third time, and that is when it came into focus.

About thirty yards to my left along the water's edge, something didn't fit the "place." A branch stuck out from the water's edge at an unnatural angle. I was drawn back to it and then noticed it was my old hunting friend. I chuckled and said, "Hello" out loud. He ignored me for awhile, and then as I spoke to him of the lovely day, he sunk his beak and neck further into his shoulders as if to say, "oh man! it's you, that 'flatlander' summer person from Connecticut in the red Jeep...ugh." He stood in the reeds like an angry old man and turned his back to me, trying his best to ignore me without giving up his prime fishing spot. If he had sighed, I wouldn't have been surprised! The great hunter of northern waterways was my swimming neighbor.....The Great Blue Heron. Surely it wasn't his last day of swimming! But, he too will be confronted with my dilemma before he wings southward!

And today was likely my last swim of 2003.

DONNIE MEETS BAMBI

Dateline: May 10, 2004

This past weekend I took Mike's puppy "Donnie" down to the cabin for an early morning "sniff" and cup of coffee. Donnie is an adorable and rambunctious Bichon who wasn't that keen on sitting on my lap and waiting for nature to come calling! I brought a biscuit or two to help him settle and accept the sentinel role. His nose twitched just as Max's used to do during similar drills with Cody. As I have written before, you just never know what, when or if you will see anything. My expectations were low. Just as I had that thought, I noticed a movement on the opposite bank of the beaver pond.......wouldn't you know! It was a doe who blended in completely, wearing her darkish winter coat that matched the bark of the sugar maples and the grey granite boulders strewn around during the Ice Age. In fact, a few times when she stopped, I lost her completely until she moved again. By the twitching of Donnie's nose and his forward lean, I knew he had either picked up the scent or could see her. He didn't growl or bark or wiggle.....he was all eyes and nose and leaning forward in my lap.

Then I noticed another movement and a fawn with a similar winter coat moved nearby the mom. Both were browsing the new spring cover. They continued to linger....which was great....since most prior sightings have been brief as they would move right out of sight into deeper woods. The doe would occasionally look over her shoulder towards us, but not directly at us. I assumed she had picked up our scent and was checking us over. This seemed odd to me, because if that were the case why did she linger, why not just move away? That question had an answer shortly as another doe appeared from the direction of the first doe.....then she turned, and she had another fawn with her! So at this point we had a front row seat on four gentle souls doing what comes naturally. Quite fitting for Mother's Day weekend! They entertained us for 20 minutes and then three of them departed stage left, ambling off. The fourth, a fawn, came down to the waterfront and began to wander over towards us. He or she got within 20 yards from us in the brush and must have picked up our scent as he/she began giving a gentle whistle/snort. Donnie thought that was cool and began to have visions of a new playmate as he began to wiggle in my lap. Eventually the fawn took the same trail that "Mel" (the Moose) had taken (in a previous Tale) and ambled off to the near left side of the scene.....A fine sighting!

Just as soon as the deer left, the "stealth fighter" birds (a/k/a Wood ducks) landed quietly and quickly in the middle of the beaver pond, hardly making a splash. There were two pair whom I hope have taken up residency in the wood duck boxes. Interestingly they were joined by one unhappy "sharp-shinned hawk" who began to bother the male wood ducks, who would have none of it. The confrontation ended as a standoff and the hawk departed stage left. I had never seen that type of argument before. Again, another interesting encounter with our fine-feathered friends!

LADY SLIPPER LANE

Dateline: June 2, 2004

What is it about holiday weekends? Does Nature wake up and bite us or do we see things more clearly with the extra time....hmmm?

Around this time of year, I always peek around the north side of the cabin to see if our patch of Lady Slippers have bloomed again. Over the last many years, I always have had one to six in bloom. This year it appears to be zippo (not the lighter)! What a bummer. As I looked and looked and looked, I did spot a tiny trillium....a great find but not enough to make up for the missing Lady Slippers.

Having been shut out in the Lady Slipper department at the cabin, I decided to stretch my viewing boundaries. My backup location is down by the Pond where I began to find one or two along the road over the past few years. I decided to make a closer inspection to satisfy my viewing bounty. Two weekends ago, Louise and I drove by and counted a stunning 28 Lady Slippers between Shaun's cabin on the road near the old one-room schoolhouse. This discovery was stunning. We've decided to call this stretch of road "Lady Slipper Lane."

This past weekend I had to make a run to the store to pick up the *Boston Globe* so I could check out the Red

Sox results. I had plenty of time and no need to rush, so I really slowed down and did a close inventory. This stretch of dirt road and a bit down the adjoining road produced a whopping 41 Slippers....surely a new World's record!......(please correct me if I am wrong!).....and all viewed from the Jeep, no poking around on foot! Being ever mindful of nature's bounty, I decided to further stretch the count from our farm to the main road, using our dirt road....that tally yielded a gorgeous 53 Lady Slippers (that includes the 41 found in Lady Slipper Lane).

And who's counting? We are! This Lady Slipper Count has become an annual event that Louise and I enjoy doing very much!

TURKEY MEETS TURKEYS

Dateline: April 25, 2005

April in the New Hampshire woods is cold to cool, normally wet, with very little sign of spring! The first sign of spring is usually found in the sounds of birds and bird migrations. My first brief encounter with spring in the New Hampshire woods this year came on April 17th. As I approached the cabin, I spotted what looked like a snowball in the water on the far side. From prior years I knew it was most probably either a frozen snowball sitting in the water (unlikely) or a male Hooded Merganser! I only saw it for a few seconds and then it disappeared into the brushy edge of the pond. Spring had arrived at the cabin!

The following Saturday morning I arrived a little later than usual at the cabin. The pond had a used dishwater look as some ducks had been cavorting prior to my arrival. No duck or other wild life was in sight. That was a good thing, as I had planned on checking/cleaning the two Wood Duck boxes and spreading some cracked corn. Cracked corn is like jumbo shrimp cocktails for any duck worth its salt! I waded out to the first box, unscrewed the hinged front door and checked for any eggshells from last year's brood. There were none. I did find and removed a large wasp's nest from the prior year and then re-screwed the door shut. Next, I proceeded to

144

circle the pond and check the beavers' dam. I always marvel at the repair work those animals perform. There were some fresh twigs, which indicated that the pond has an active beaver colony. Along the way, I cast some cracked corn so the ducks would make a delightful discovery on their next landing. I got down to the dam itself and inspected the fine detail work of the repairs. As I turned to retrace my steps back to the cabin, a head popped up from the brush about 15 feet away. Obviously he and I were quite startled! The head looked exactly like that Nature Conservancy logo that they use on their pre-addressed labels sent out with fund-raising efforts. The head staring at me had a neck easily 3 feet tall, with a long beak and a very evil eye! I wasn't entirely sure whether or not it was going to chase me!! Then I realized it had heard me and smelled the cracked corn as it hit the water and the leaves nearby. He likely smelled it and wanted in on the feast! The head belonged to a four-foot-tall Tom turkey that was traveling with a harem of 3 hens. They couldn't decide whether to come towards me for the corn or fly away. They finally decided to wander away. This was the first time I had seen turkeys at the cabin "up close and personal!"

I returned to the cabin and decided to circle the pond to the south, cross the footbridge and check out the Wood Duck box on the west side of the pond. The footing was slick and I used my walking stick to avoid falling into the pond. I stopped about 15 yards from the second Wood Duck box and spread some cracked corn. I then took one more step to the Wood Duck box and suddenly, out wiggled Ms. Merganser from the box and quietly swooped away towards the dam. She was a pretty sight even if she didn't have the coloration that the snowball male has! I was probably more startled than she was and began to worry that I may have scared her from her roost permanently. That would be a shame as the Wood Duck box is a swell location to bring 10 to 13 ducklings into the world. I stopped dead in my tracks and retraced my steps back to the cabin. The inspection/cleaning of the second Wood Duck box would have to wait 'til next fall or winter. As I crossed the footbridge, I spotted a rather pleasant scene up the brook. There was a beautiful mountain waterfall nestled in the moss and evergreens. It was a picture of peacefulness and serenity! I couldn't help but think of how much Louise and I wish that a few of our close friends who are in tough places could absorb the serenity of that stream scene.

I sat on the cabin porch and waited to see if Ms. Merganser would return to the box. About 15 minutes later, on a fresh breeze from the north, a Great Blue Heron plopped down directly in front of me. He also had a neck 3 feet long and also gave me the evil eye. I had a pair of binocs on my chest and thought I could bring them up to study the beast! Wrong! As soon as I undid my hands, the Great Blue gingerly flapped his wings, leaned forward and glided away to the north! Skunked again!!

Postscript: On Sunday morning I returned to the cabin in an oblique manner. The brook was flooded as it had rained all night and the paths were full of puddles, so I circled to the cabin using the highest ground I could find. As I approached the cabin, I spotted a beaver moving near the dam. The water was moving fast through the pond and all was quiet! I drank my coffee and waited about a half hour when, Poof!...on a south breeze Ms. Merganser glided into the center of the pond. She circled to a dead log and preened herself there. I didn't move a muscle, as I did not want to see her flee from me again. Eventually after circling in the water looking for Mr. Merganser, she lifted off and flew to and into the Wood Duck box on the far side of the pond!

All's well that ends well!

THEATER IN THE WILD

"NO VACANCY"

A new one-act play by Yours Truly, written on location in New Hampshire, April 2005. The play recounts the struggle of two couples to meet their domestic needs and find shelter in the deep dark forest.

Cast in Order of Appearance

Warbler
Canada Geese (heard off stage)
Mr. and Mrs. Wood Duck
"Trent" Trout as ripples in the water
Marissa Merganser
"Bucky" Beaver
"Hairy" Heron
Phyllis Phoebe
"Blackie" Black Cap Chickadee
Audience of one

ACT I

Preamble

The Play begins with "HC" trudging along the trail to his beaver dam in the mist of a dark, damp early

morning dawn. He has packed some cracked corn, his walking stick and his trusty cup of coffee. As he passes from meadow number one into the woodlot before the Beaver pond, he hears the distinct and sweet sound of a Warbler trilling away in the morning's wooded amphitheater. It's a welcome sound to early fishermen, but usually heard later in the summer.

"HC" creeps up to "The Theater in the Wild" by using the log cabin as a blind/shield from the critters in and around the pond. However, there comes a moment when he must "show" himself briefly before sliding around to the front porch and into his pre-paid season seat.

The Curtain Rises!

Scene I

The stage at first glance is un-remarkable. Woods, water and mist.....no movement, no critters and very little sound, only an occasional Canada Goose from the pond down stream a bit. The coffee is still warm and the "opera glasses/binocs" uncover nothing. All is still as still can be.

Perhaps this will be yet another "skunked morning" venture!

Time passes......By some it is counted by ticks; however, HC doesn't put much truck in the concept of time at such moments......it's really all relative! Tick....Tick....Tick.

Scene II

Stage right..........a subtle ripple on the water foretells an arrival. Shortly thereafter, Mr. and Mrs. Wood Duck paddle close to the near edge, perhaps in search of last week's cracked corn castings. Words cannot describe the beauty of young Wood Ducks; they have such magnificent coloration. HC studied each using his opera glasses, as this was the first sighting for 2005. They wander a bit and eventually meander to the far shore. Middle stage, another ripple in the pond; however, there was no creature to be seen. At first, HC suspects a Beaver submarine would breach the surface, but no.....it must be Trent Trout surfacing and nibbling near the middle of the former brook bed.

As HC studies the far bank and the Woodies, his ear picks up a croak reminiscent of a Raven's mid-flight occasional croak. He looks up into the tree tops/ floodlights and searches for the wandering Raven.....none to be found! Tiring of the search, he turns his eyes to the pond and is delighted and surprised to see Marissa Merganser paddling around the far side while croaking to her mate. Once again her mate is not to be found. Now, Marissa has set up her apartment in the far Wood Duck box for several weeks and HC suspects she feels threatened by the new couple paddling at the base of her dwelling. "Where is a good man when you need one?" was likely going through her and HC's mind.

Finally, in a huff, she departs gliding gracefully stage right!

Scene III

No sooner has Marissa departed stage right when "Bucky" Beaver glides in from stage right....almost a ballet move.....His "nose to tail tip" must be close to three feet. Clearly, Bucky is long in the tooth! He looks like a scale model of the Russian Sub in *The Hunt for Red October*. He glides to center stage and waddles up onto a small grass/twig/mud island and begins his monologue of noise. Upon dry land he looks like a hairy bowling ball with head and all teeth.

His gourmet selection is composed of a leafy twig of a tender shoot and lime green foliage. He snaps it off at the base and begins to chatter it into his mouth like a grinding blade in a Home Depot chipping machine. It echoes around the pond! He looks lost in the moment.

Seconds later, stage right, in glides "Hairy" Heron again and sets up shop within spitting distance of "Bucky." In fact, it looks to me like Hairy was eating some of the crumbs "Bucky" was leaving behind. Now Hairy is a splendid sight and appears regal with a white plume and cocked tuff of hair in his crest-line. It always amazes me when different species tolerate one another's presence.

The stage is quite crowded with the Woodies in the far side eyeing Marissa's apartment; Hairy and Bucky feasting on fresh growth mid-pond; and then several Phoebes, who have selected the cabin as their nest, begin bombing around. An occasional "Black Capped" Chickadee flits to and fro, making selections from the bark of the white pines.

Scene IV

Hairy tires and glides away stage right.

Bucky tires and glides away stage right, followed by a crash dive, accompanied by a canon ball flap of his tail as he descends to the safety of the dam (off stage). The sound is identical to throwing a boulder into the middle of a pond.

In the meantime, the Woodies wander to the near front stage and resume the search for cracked corn. They come within 15 feet of the audience and pretend not to notice HC. Mrs. Woodie begins to eye the nearby wood duck box. She makes her way over to it and her mate follows. It appears to the audience that she is apartment hunting and asking herself, "Will this one do?" She proceeds to fly/hop up onto its short roofline and bend over to check to see if it's watertight! Eventually she tires, hop/flies down and exits stage right.

The audience wonders why she doesn't go into the box. Is it because it doesn't meet her standard or perhaps because another Woodie is in residence?

Perhaps the owner should start using "NO VACANCY" signs.

The curtain falls and the audience applauds!

"CABIN INTERRUPTUS"

Dateline: August 22, 2005

Prologue:
Louise: "You're back early!?"
Hank: "How do you spell NOIR?"

The Tale

It was a glum, overcast damp Saturday morning as I meandered down to the cabin. The woods were quiet with a stillness that often begins to happen in August as time starts to stand still in southern New Hampshire. I picked my favorite way over limbs and twigs so that any noise would be muted. As I approached the cabin, my familiar saying rang in my head, "You either see something right away or you need to wait till it comes into your zone." As the thought bubbled out of my head, I saw the rear end of a very black animal scoot away from me dead center in the beaver pond. As he departed, I assumed I had somehow spooked him into such motion. I now know that was not necessarily the case. A pang of excitement rushed through me, as my sighting was the rear end of a black bear, perhaps our own "Guy Noir"....Louise's appellation of the local black bear named after the famous character in Garrison Keillor's

154

"Private Eye" sketch on "Prairie Home Companion!" My first reaction was, damn! I wish I had somehow moved more slowly or quietly so I could actually see Guy Noir in action, doing his thing!

As I started to take another step forward, I was startled to see Mr. Noir come around behind a small island of tall grass in the pond. Apparently I had not spooked him at all; in fact, he didn't yet know I was present! He was just meandering this damp morning. I froze, coffee mug in hand. Then I immediately turned into that famous former granite "Old Man of the Mountain" of New Hampshire fame! Mr. Noir slid into the chilly brook up to his nose and began to swim. Clearly, Mr. Noir was a "sinker," an athletic sinker! He paddled a few yards with only his nose showing, heading for the muddy bank of the dam that crosses the brook and is about 50 yards long. He clawed his way up the bank using some dead limbs for leverage, as the embankment was very slippery. He stood on the grassy part of the bank and shook himself, much like Cody (our beloved Golden Retriever) used to do after a dip. I got a good look at him...he was the size of a very, very large Black lab and very athletic. When he shook himself, the muscles and skin moved easily about his backside and the water chased the leaves above him.

I was on the horns of a dilemma now....what to do? Stay and study or back off and miss Guy's show? What to do? What to do? As I was turning this thought over in my head, Mr. Noir strolled a few paces along the bank and lifted his nose skyward. I thought, oh damn!

He's got my scent; I'd better go….Again I struggled with the "fight or flee" genes. I decided to study him one more time before I gave him the slip. As I peered across the grassy pond, maybe 30 yards away, I thought, Oh My Gosh! There's a second one! But I was wrong. Mr. Noir was now standing on his hind legs with his back to me, and his arms fully extended up to the top of the blueberry bushes which grow atop the beaver dam bank. I would estimate he was between 5 and 6 feet tall. But why was he standing?

Again I debated, go or stay? As the seconds flew by, I saw him embrace 5 or 6 bush limbs and draw them to his chest and then very gracefully lean them to the ground. He pivoted as he did this, so when he was done, he was then facing me with the bouquet of bush limbs under his body and the tops of the bush flopping up around his large hairy head. This was pure Black Bear Blueberry picking! The picture reminded me of how Cody would hold a large bone between his paws while he munched away. I could clearly see his big head chomping away from sprig to sprig. So often the cabin scene is still, quiet and empty; however, today it was as if Clark Gable had magically appeared in a black Tuxedo and slicked back black hair with a twinkle in his eye and that smirk in his grin……Guy Noir indeed!

I suspected he would be chomping a fair bit; however, his face and alignment put me directly in his line of sight. Either his eyes or his nose was bound to pick me up any second. I decided to retreat for another day. After all, this was his place, his time, not my bird feeder or my trash can. This was au natural, so enjoy your breakfast, Mr. Noir! I'll enjoy my quiet coffee time another day!

And now Louise, how do you spell Noir?

"THE YOUNG AND THE CURIOUS"

Dateline: August 8, 2005

I had finished my coffee and blueberry muffin on the porch of the cabin. I was trying to decide whether to pick more blueberries or head to the dump for my Saturday ritual. It has been a great year for blueberries and the farm has been producing some really fine muffins thanks to Louise. As I sat there, I finally decided to wait another 5 minutes "just in case." As I waited, a hummingbird buzzed the empty/near-empty feeder. Damn! I had meant to bring a refill of Louise's homemade sugar nectar down to refill it. As the hummer buzzed off, I thought I noticed a look of disgust on his face.

Quietly, to my right I saw a small deer's head arrive above the tall grass at water's edge. A "Bambi" was about to enter my sphere, much like "Mel" did a few years earlier. I swear his young ears were bigger than his head and he/she was the size of a skinny Golden Retriever. Slowly Bambi minced her way to the front of the porch about 20 yards away. In hindsight, I suspect she was edging over to my blueberry patch to snack away. She kept on looking at me (and I was frozen stiff) and sniffing the air. From her head movement, I was sure she really didn't see me or hear me, so her primary radar was her nose. I was tempted to say "Good morning,

Doll." However, since she was under a year, I suspect that the mere tone of my voice would freak her out, so I remained still, very still. She got to be dead center in front of me and then her nose or genes took over. I couldn't tell whether her fear gene said, "Look out! men at work" or whether her nose said "hmmmm, nice muffin and coffee!" Either way (or both), she came to a stop and resisted the mighty blueberry snack temptation! She shook her head and wheeled and returned to stage right from whence she had entered. She then stopped and turned around to begin the dance again!

Back she came to center stage; however, this time she made it a point to stamp her left front foot with authority....I recall that is a signal for something I've forgotten. Just before she got to the center, the young hummingbird returned full of attitude and then dropped down within a foot of my bright red golf cap and hovered there, checking me out. Ok, I thought, so I look like a big red-topped carnation. So what? Then it occurred to me that this hummer was serious. I fully expected he would approach my cap or my eyeballs to check for nectar. The latter would not be good! So I was on the horns of a dilemma....do I make a motion to dispatch the hummer or let the little devil put his long beak into somewhere I didn't want it? What to do?....as Bambi was making her last few steps to center stage.

I must do something and quick.....so I opened my mouth and gently blew some hot air out towards the hummer without making any other physical moves. The hummer got the message real quick and buzzed off in a big huff! Bambi, on the other hand, was once again having second thoughts. She turned her head back towards the dam where I suspect Mom was browsing. Nope, she couldn't finish the deal.... and so she wheeled back to stage right. She stopped and did the grown-up deer snort three times....so cute to see! I've heard the adult snort many times and Bambi had it down pat! Finally, she quickly moved further stage right to re-join Mom.

Time to head to the dump!

"WAITING TO EXHALE"

Dateline: May, 2006

May 2006 had its own version of "Cabin fever." Rain seems to be the order of the weekends and it had extended into June! My trip to the cabin now required "Wellingtons" and work gloves. I jokingly had referred to the local wildlife staying in their own log cabins! I haven't written a "Cabin Tale" in 2006, so I decided to dedicate the first one to "rain in the woods" sans animals.

As I stepped down the path to the cabin, I was focused on the touch and feel of the cold drizzle and tried to reflect on how to describe it. The best I could come up with was that icy cold drip of water that hits the back of your neck as you move under a drip line without an umbrella! That describes May 2006, at least on weekends! I slowed to pick a path around the first large puddle, when I saw a flash of movement about 20 yards away. I had "jumped" a yearling! His first step seems more like a fall to the right or left as they tuck their front legs under and spring with their hind legs. The dodge move was totally instinctive, as if to avoid an arrow or musket ball.

The yearling danced about 10 yards and then stopped to look back over its shoulder. I had already frozen in my tracks and remained so. I've learned that young deer tend to be more curious than "old bucks." We remained locked in a "Mexican standoff" and I knew I could outlast the yearling. Sure 'nuff, he moved to get a better view back. Five minutes went by and then he snorted (loud exhale) and bolted another 10 yards. This snort is quite typical, and I had heard it many times before and actually anticipated it. However, in a flash I decided I would also snort myself as a near imitation. When I snorted using my best imitation, the yearling stopped dead, turned and wandered back about 10 yards with its ears twitching. He snorted again and so did I. We both stood there snorting at one another. To this day, I don't have a clue what I was saying, but the yearling was fully engaged to find out.

He turned and walked parallel to the path I was taking, so I walked forward as well. He'd turn and look at me, and I'd turn and look at him. If he snorted, I'd snort. I decided to have some more fun with him and waited until I passed behind a particularly large tree and hid behind it. I'd peek to see his hindquarter, then I'd stay hidden. He didn't know what to do except crane his head this way and that to see if he could spot me. We played this form of tag for several more minutes. I eventually grew tired and broke off down the path to the cabin, smirking to myself as if to say, "Who's the 'old buck' now?"

The cabin was damp; the woods were wet; the drizzle was falling and the beaver dam was overflowing!

Postscript: On Sunday, the annual "Lady Slipper" count was held. A new world's record was achieved obliterating last year's total of 116. Louise and Hank tallied an even 200! (The current record is over 500 set in 2010!)

"MIRACLE IN THE MEADOW," MEMORIAL DAY 2008

Dateline: May 14, 1989

This tale starts on my birthday on May 14, 1989. Louise has given me a beautiful birthday gift of an apple tree of my choice for my 48th birthday. I have chosen a blooming Macintosh. I was thrilled with this generous gift, as I have wanted to re-populate the farm's meadow with some fruit trees.

When I was a child, the farm had an old ailing apple orchard with about 25 or so semi-dead, lumbering, falling and failing trees. Unfortunately, the orchard was not a pretty sight. My Dad gave me the task to clean it up, meaning cut them down and haul the dead trees and limbs away. I was about 10 years old and up to the task, or so I thought. I jumped at the job and had a self-image of Paul Bunyan without "Babe, the Blue Ox." I can still remember the thrill of being given my own first smallish axe and let loose to clear the Orchard.

My enthusiasm lasted most of the morning of the first day! By about 11 a.m., my hands were raw and bloody with new calluses. I wasn't tired and still wanted to get going; however, I had only dented the first inch of an old apple tree with my dull, hand-forged, smallish axe found in the corner of what we now call "The Magic

Shed." About that time my Dad decided to check on my progress. I now believe he knew perfectly well how I would fare. In any case, he staged "surprise" at my apparent lack of progress and chided me to get going, as I had a long way to go and then he left. I did continue; stopped for lunch (peanut butter and marshmallow sandwich and an orange syrup soda drink). Once back at it I was able to get the first tree to tilt over, but not cut through. I was feeling proud, with one down (sort of) and 24 to go. This was Man stuff, and I looked forward to my parents' approval as all kids do. My Dad re-checked my progress and shook his head and muttered something about my having a long way to go. My Mom took pity on me and provided some rag tag gloves to help the bleeding hands. She also approached my Dad with some discussion about the dullness of the axe head I had to use. Midafternoon my Dad stopped in the meadow, gave me a file, and said maybe I needed it to sharpen the blade, as it might help. Of course I had never seen a hand file and had no idea how to "sharpen an axe blade," but I was all for anything to help me move to tree number 2. My brother, Herb, was probably helping my Dad build the huge fieldstone fireplace in our current bedroom, I suspect. He never made it to the meadow the first day to taunt me. Later that night he laughed at me when I tried to sharpen the axe blade, but was drawing the file in an incorrect direction so the blade was no sharper after my effort than before. Eventually he showed me the principle of how to do it. The second day I was able to finish the first tree and it was one of the smaller ones….ugh!

And so my summer of discontent proceeded. Eventually, my hands hardened, I got the knack of a sharp blade and what it could do, and my skinny frame became wiry, if not strong. I finished the season eliminating 21 of the 25 trees and learned just how tough apple wood really is. It did keep me out of my Dad's hair, as he and my brother tried to finish the huge fireplace. And I am sure my Dad knew I would gain some values from knowing what hard physical labor can contribute to a young man's growth. My hands never were soft again and I have always valued what a sharp blade can do on any job around the farm or in the woods!

By 1989, I was glad I had left three trees in the meadow, way up at the top. They still bear fruit and no one knows what type they are. I began to think I'd like to add more young apple trees to the meadow I had partially denuded as a child, hence the Macintosh choice for my birthday!

The 1989 tree had a huge root ball and weighed more than what one man could lift. I needed help to plant it and waited until Memorial Day for the help from family and their friends. As I recall, Mike and Kelly came up with Liz and a friend from UCONN (who hailed from Wisconsin.). Kate and Christian were also there. I had a lot of free "dude labor"! It was an adventure to assemble, kick them off the porch, find the tools, and actually begin to wrestle the beast into the ground. They were all good sports and when we were done, Louise took a photo of the entire "dude labor crew." We still have the photo somewhere in a box of others at the farm.

Later that summer I decided to unwrap the white plastic shield tape which had been spun around the trunk to protect it in transport, or so I thought. As I unwrapped the tape I was horrified to see that the tape hid an enormous and deadly gash - dead center in the trunk about 10 inches long and quite deep. I suspected the tree might not live. I was already very fond of that tree and hoped that if it might make it through the winter, the gash would self heal and the Macintosh would fruit in all its glory. But deep inside I was quite worried that all of that was wishful thinking. I had to wait till the next spring to see if my faith in that tree would be served.

The following spring the Macintosh had leaves but no blooms. By mid-summer it was struggling and the ends of some of the limbs were dying bit by bit. By fall it was a mess, and barely alive. I hoped a new spring would grant some fresh re-growth and new hope for "tree self actualization"!

The following spring I was horrified to find that local starving deer had nipped all the new fresh growth in order to survive a harsh winter. Such is life in the New Hampshire woods in the winter. I couldn't fault the deer and ached for the tree. Again, it was a struggle for it to make it through the growing season. By fall, it was a mess again. A small sprout began growing at the ground line, as often happens with most fruit trees. Most folks clip these off, but I didn't, as it signaled some inter tree strength and I was pulling for it any way the tree could survive. The next year the tree again greened up and was chomped by the local deer; however, the sprout fared

167

well and grew about 2 feet along side the 5-foot trunk, a slender reminder of what might be if the trunk were healthy. By fall, the tree had slipped into a coma. I decided to wait to the following spring and cut it out permanently. Spring came and I approached the near-dead tree and proceeded to consider where to cut. I noticed that the sprout remained healthy again and was 3 feet tall; the size of a pencil. I had no trouble removing the original dead trunk but I couldn't bring myself to cut the sprout. So I decided to do just that, cut the dead trunk and leave the sprout and say a prayer for the sprout, as I really expected it not to remain alive the following spring.

There it was the next spring, a pencil sized three-foot sprout with a handful of leaves looking kind of silly as an orchard "wannabe." A few friends would smile and humor me about my great big orchard tree but I didn't care. That sprout deserved a chance and *The Little Engine That Could* was my favorite childhood book. Louise let me down gently and told me that even if it did survive, it likely would never have fruit as the sprout came from only half of the hybrid graft. By then I didn't really care if it was barren as long as it was green and pretty. We helped it along that year by hanging bags of Cody's fur in small pantyhose pouches so the deer would not chomp the little champ. Louise continued to give it fertilizer year after year.

And so the years flew by and the sprout began to take a shape of its own and eventually got to the size of the original gift tree. I was thrilled one day to find out from Bill S. that he had done the same kind of thing successfully with some nut tree. That gave me hope that at least I would have a lovely "green only" barren apple tree. 1989, 90, 91, 92……and on and on clicked by.

And then we come to Memorial Day, 2008! My special effort tree greets another new year. A few days before the actual Memorial Day, Louise came down from the garden where the tree grows modestly and said I had to sit down, as she had some very special news to share with me. I sat down in the screened-in front porch and awaited her news. Such news usually unglues me a bit, as you just never know! She said, "Your special tree has blooms this year!" You could have knocked me over with a feather. We couldn't believe our eyes. Sure enough, the tree is full of blooms for the first time since 1989……19 years! We both feel it is a miracle tree and it reminded me once again of one my father's favorite sayings, "Keep the faith."

Happy Memorial Day!

"LIVE FREE AND FLY"

Dateline: Father's Day 2008

Somehow, it seems fitting to write this tale on a Father's Day (or a Mother's Day). Over the years, the farm and the cabin have been a host site for nesting Phoebes. Each spring we'd arrive on a Friday night to find a nest begun, either on the eves of the front porch or on a shelf above the windows of the back porch. The activity would be intense as both the mom and dad would first build the nest and then (after the hatch) they'd switch to hunter mode to feed the "young'uns." The primary feed for the chicks would be the dreaded "black flies," so you can see why the Phoebes are an easy bird to love as they drift around the yard or cabin picking off the nasty black flies!

The only downside of the nest would be the accompanying bird droppings that slightly stain the Fitzwilliam green porch frame. Each year I'd have to wash the stain and then repaint the offending site....a very small price to pay for the annual Phoebe ritual. The Phoebe is a lovely and gentle bird which seems to balance itself by flicking its tail as it sits on a phone wire, fence post, or Adirondack chair by the "Pit." I am always comforted by the fact that more mouths to feed means fewer flies to bite me. The typical brood can be 6 to 10.

We can never figure out how they all fit into the nest prior to flight. In the beginning, it seems to be a nest of mouths all craning and chirping for Mom and Dad to attend to their hunger. Eventually they grow to fill the nest and overflow onto each other, shoulder to shoulder, waiting for that famous moment of leaving the nest! Each babe would try to gather the courage to fly, usually waiting for a sibling to go first. Each Friday night we'd arrive to one, or perhaps two, fewer babes in the nest and know the right amount of courage had been summoned until eventually all were gone to their new sites.

Several weeks ago, I wandered down to the cabin to attend the annual cabin "open up." I usually button it down for winter and return in the spring to unlock and flip up the window cover on the front porch. This year I noticed some white bird stain by the porch corner to the cabin. I knew without looking that a Phoebe couple had once again selected the cabin for its king-sized birdhouse. Good choice. I unlocked the door and peeked in to see what if any carnage occurred over the nasty winter months. Oh yes, the local redneck squirrels had their usual "frat" party and tipped over anything tip-able and pitched their beer cans and potato chip bags all over the floor. They do know how to throw a monster bash each year, it seems.

After cleaning up their mess, I settled into the rocker on the front porch to assess the local scene. It was a quiet and lovely sunny day. The beaver pond was quite full from the spring melt-off and everything was greening out. No animals in sight, but plenty of bird sounds. A very pleasant scene indeed, at least for awhile. After about 10 minutes of pleasant solitude, I began to notice Mr. and Mrs. Phoebe approaching me near the porch, flitting from nearby pine limb to pine limb. It became quite clear they were not fond of my arrival, and were letting me know that in no uncertain terms. Nothing very aggressive, but showing me their irritation by jumping and chirping well within eyesight. Most distracting!

Suddenly a very aggressive Hummingbird flew into my face....5 inches away to assert and underscore the fact I was *persona non grata!* The hummer actually startled the daylights out of me, since I first thought it might be a huge yellow jacket! After this unsettling event, I decided that maybe I needed to make my presence known gradually over the days and weeks, and not run for mayor of the cabin on day one. And so I departed after checking out the beaver dam and our beloved dog cemetery nearby.

A week later, I returned to the cabin for a respite from "farm open up" chores. I settled in on the porch and began my survey of the pond and shores. All was quiet and well. I expected the Phoebes to quickly return to tell me off, but was pleasantly surprised that they let me relax for 15 minutes before taking up their protests. While I was absent they painted up some signs and hand bills...."Yankee go home," "Flatlanders not welcome," "Air Force Grads only" and such messages.

I knew I was going to be ridden out of town again and accepted it. I jumped off the front porch to the fire pit in front and heard an explosion above my head. I couldn't tell what it was at first, but it sounded like a Canada goose had slammed into the roof of the porch. I quickly turned to check out the expected damage. And to my surprise, I saw a scatter squawk of 10 or so baby Phoebe chicks. It seems my thud on the ground scared them all out of their nest all at once. It was like I had flushed a covey of quail, only these were mere babes in arms! Each had flitted to the nearest pine limb they could find. What was truly amusing to me was that each one seemed to have a pumped up chest like a Disney cartoon as if to say, "Look at me! I can fly like Mom and Dad! Look at me! Look at me!"

And so another great generation of Phoebes begins its life.

PETER'S DEMISE

A few weeks back as I walked the pups to the brook, I spotted Peter's figure. It seemed to cover half the dirt road near our driveway. The pups were pulling very hard to get to him!

Peter was a leviathan of a porcupine!

Clearly the largest one I had ever seen in my life.

What occurred? It seemed that perhaps a Redneck Truck Driver after too many Bud blues bumped him off with his fender upon returning late night or early morning. Peter was waddling up the hill to the farm, his safe haven, and did not make it.

After conducting a forensic investigation, it occurred to me that it was highly likely Peter and I had shared many years together and Peter likely had better green card credentials than I for living at the farm. After all, he spent the winters there and we didn't.

His paws were enormous, the size of my hands! The pads reminded me of old baseball gloves; well worn, dark and bulging. His nails needed clipping and each nail was easily the length of 1/2 of a quarter. His head was handsome and well groomed with quills everywhere. I estimated his weight to be over 40 pounds when I gave him his fitting burial.

As the reality of the event sunk in, I felt sad, but also realized he had really lived a good and long, long life. It also occurred to me that his life and mine had numerous intersections, as I believed he lived under our farmhouse. It seems fitting to recount those interactions in tribute to his time spent at Blueberry Meadow Farm.

Peter's Life at Blueberry Meadow Farm

The best way to recount his life is to tell the events in reverse order and thereby memorialize some of those event. So the most recent spotting occurred to Loyd, our general contractor, as he was doing some repair work on our back porch. Peter decided to visit him by descending onto a huge maple tree close behind Loyd. The sound of the animal descending the tree scared Loyd; however, he regained his composure and was able to record a video of the beast in action!

The winter of 2014/2015 was also a beast! Most locals have erased the bitter memory from their collective recall; however, Peter's scars remain! We did not spot him, but his marks were quite evident. It seems that Peter was in a battle of survival that winter, and food and salt had become extremely scarce under our farmhouse. I envision him waddling under the four feet of snow to the farm's front flowerbeds. His nose must have bumped into one of our transplanted Japanese Maple trees. He must have found the bark tasty, and so he removed the bark two feet up, then moved onto another Japanese maple and repeated his lunch or dinner. Later, he returned and ate the bark of some of the 1880 rose bushes. All survived except one transplanted

175

Japanese maple from Louise's former house in Connecticut. I was thrilled that the plants helped Peter make it through that ugly winter. He also appears to have found a few hemlocks in the woods near the farm to supplement his appetite. Those have not fared well either.

Several years ago when Louise and I had returned in early spring from our Florida winter, I decided to take the pups out the back room for their evening routine. As soon as I hit the concrete steps, I knew the pups had smelled or spotted Peter nearby. Both tried to rip my arms off my body to get to the great quilled one! And there in the moonlight I spotted Peter waddling away towards the woods.

On another fall weekend, I took the pups out and was surprised to see Peter on the back steps looking in at us. I opened the slider and of course he headed for the exit; however, where was the exit? We had had our leaves raked and some had blown up to the fence. Poor Peter could not find the accustomed holes in the fence. He was stuck in the back yard with the pups barking at him through the slider. I grabbed a broom and attempted to guide Peter to an exit. He was not a happy camper, but he eventually saw the wisdom of my ways and got out of Dodge! I have never seen a Porcupine move so fast once he found the opening!

I would be remiss if I did not recount the two encounters that my Golden Retrievers had with Peter. Jefferson and Cody, both off leash, found Peter near a stone wall and did what Goldens do...they typically try to bite a Porcupine. The results were not pretty, and both events were very traumatic to all involved, including Peter!

The most amusing encounter happened in the late 1970s. We were asleep upstairs in an experimental attic bedroom. Sometime around 3:00 a.m. I heard a knock at the front door....never a good thing! I clambered downstairs to answer the front door.....no one there!? So I returned to bed, and in a few minutes, I heard a knock again. This time I suspected it was at the back door. Now that was really weird. Again, I descended and opened the back door.....no one there! Disgusted, I returned to bed. Again, several minutes later I heard the knock downstairs. This time I waited to focus on the exact location. It turned out it was coming from the old privy toward the rear south end of the farmhouse. What the hell would be knocking there, I wondered! So I got a baseball bat and approached the privy with flashlight in hand as well. I put the bat down and lifted the lid and pointed the flashlight down the cavity! Low and behold, there was Peter snacking for salt in the splashboard!!!

The Burial

So you can see Peter and I go way back, and in my sadness I felt he deserved a proper and fitting country burial. I shouldered him on the shovel and waddled down to the brook. There is a cut on the south side of the brook which I have used for planting extra day lilies. I placed Peter on the ground and dug a large hole and placed him therein. I spotted a huge boulder nearby and rolled it on top of the fresh grave.

Rest in peace old friend Peter.

5

❀ ❀ ❀

Farm Firsts &
Life Lists

FARM FIRSTS

The following list represents various "Firsts" associated with the farm.

First Settlers, Peter Holbrook and Lydia Darling Holbrook purchased land (roughly 200 acres) on November 11, 1763. They and one child likely moved to the site from Cumberland Rhode Island.

Peter Holbrook attended the first town meeting in the 1760's.

Peter Holbrook was the Town's first "Petit Juror" in 1760's.

Peter and Lydia had 11 more children born at the farm. Birth records show births every other year for at least 22 years with no deaths.

Peter Holbrook went to the defense of Fort Ticonderoga in 1776 from the farm. Lydia's nephew, Caleb Thayer, died at the Battle of the Cedars near Montreal, the Town's first casualty of the Revolutionary War. The Thayer's farm was next west to the Holbrook farm, now a cellar hole.

The first cultivated white roses arrived in 1880 and are planted near our front mail box (the first Rural Delivery-style mailbox.)

Arthur Perry acquired the first "Abenaque" gas operated mobile lumber sawmill in the late 1890s.

Arthur Perry acquired the first Ford Model "T" in 1914. It still runs and visits the farm, driven by his son or grandson.

In 1938 the farm was connected to the first battery-operated telephone "farm to farm" system.

In 1947, Jerry and Louise Hallas acquired the farm as first non-resident owners.

Electricity arrived in 1952 due to the Rural Electrification Act;

Hot running water was added shortly thereafter in 1952.

Jerry Hallas built a fieldstone fireplace in 1955 and 1956.

A modern phone system, complete with hard-wired AT&T wall phone arrived in the early 1960's.

My parents tried propane heating in the late 1960's, abandoned in 1970's.

Hank and Louise added a new living room and porch to the rear of the structure in 1993.

Hank and Louise Hallas added the first oil heating system in 1994.

In 1995, Hank rebuilt the outdoor fireplace, forever called "The Pit" on the site of the original cabin dwelling.

The original 20-foot deep dug well lasted from 1760's until 2000 when Hank and Louise had a 400-foot deep drilled well installed, along with a water line up to the garden area.

Occasional use of a small TV began in 1970's and the first full-time satellite TV arrived in 2006.

Internet arrived via satellite in 2007.

LIFE LISTS: ANIMALS

The following lists of animal life are a compilation of over 60 years of observations with my own eyes on and around the "Blueberry Meadow Farm."

Large Mammals
Moose
White Tailed Deer
Horses (various)
Black Bear
Gray Wolf
Black Panther
Bob Cat
Fisher Cat
Coyote
River Otter
Red Fox
Sheep
Oxen
Cows
Dogs

Medium Mammals
Beaver
Woodchuck
Snowshoe Hare

Eastern Cottontail
Skunk
Raccoon
Mink
Weasel
Porcupine
Opossum
Farm Pig

Small Animals
Grey Squirrel
Red Squirrel
Flying Squirrel
Brown Bat
House Mouse
Vole
Chipmunk a/k/a "Monk"
Shrew
Mole
Box Turtle
Snapping Turtle
Wood Turtle
Bull Frog
Horned Frog
Leopard Frog
Corn Snake
Garter Snake
Black Racer

Fish
Brook Trout
Brown Trout
Bullheads
Shiners
Pan Fry
Bass
Pickerels
Perch

LIFE LIST: BIRDS

Birds Seen in and Around the Farm over the Years

Merganser
Barn Swallow
Great Blue Heron
Black Duck
Mallard
Canada Geese
Ruby Throated Hummingbird
Hummingbird
Green Heron
Little Blue Heron
Turkey Vulture
Sharp-shinned Hawk
Cooper's Hawk
Red-Shouldered Hawk
Red-Tailed Hawk
Bald Eagle
Osprey
American Kestrel
Peregrine Falcon
Ruffed Grouse
Bobwhite
Ring Necked Pheasant
Turkey

Woodcock
Sandpiper Upland
Pigeon
Mourning Dove
Barred Owl
Saw-whet
Great Horned Owl
Snowy Owl
Whip-poor-will
Nighthawk
Flicker
Pileated Woodpecker
Red Bellied Woodpecker
Yellow Bellied Sapsucker
Hairy Woodpecker
Downy Woodpecker
Purple Martin
Blue Jay
Raven
Crow
Tufted Titmouse
Nuthatch
House Wren
Catbird
Brown Thrasher
Hermit Thrush
Vireo
Eastern Bluebird
Cedar Waxwing
Starling

American Redstart
Bobolink
Red-winged Blackbird
Oriole
Grackle
Cowbird
Scarlet Tanager
Cardinal
Grosbeak
Purple Finch
Yellow Finch

2001 BEAVER POND BIRD CENSUS BY LEWIS

Dateline: June 22, 2001

To: Hank Hallas
From: Lewis
Subject: Birds

I can't remember when I participated in such a bird-watching expedition as yesterday! I went up to your cabin to see the young Mergansers. Such plush chairs. (old rockers) I spent about one hour there. You probably are interested in what I saw/heard. They are not in scientific order but this is what I can think of tonight 36 hours later (plus one Gin and Tonic):

Dark eyed Junco
Tree Swallow
Belted Kingfisher
Red Winged Black Bird
Phoebe
Flicker
Goldfinch
Wilson's Warbler
Chestnut-Sided Warbler
Pine Warbler

Red eye Vireo
Solitary Vireo
Starling
Common Grackle
White Throated Sparrow
Black Capped Chickadee
Robin
Hermit Thrush
One Wood duck with six young ones about 6" long
No Mergansers

PET LIST

The following is a list of Pets who have loved the farm since we acquired it.

"Monkey"
A Dandie Dinmont Terrier, our first family pet that among other achievements was smuggled into and then out of Canada.

"Spic and Span"
Twin Beagles who would run forever and were often relegated to a long Tobacco wire run in the back meadow and across the street where the cars are parked. Spic was the bright one and he belonged to Herb. I was the custodian of Span who was most lovable if not too bright. ;)

"Twiggy"

Twiggy was a Cairn terrier belonging to my mother who loved him dearly. He was fearless and possessive.

"Tigger"

A calico cat that had been abandoned in the Park River when we lived in Hartford. She was Queen of the roost at the farm.ʹ

"Jefferson"

Jefferson was my first Golden Retriever, a much loved, lovable, and loyal dog. He had two nasty run-ins with Porcupines, among other adventures.

"Curly"

Curly was my second Golden Retriever and a true free spirit who was my great pal when I was single. He was named for a golden lock of hair on his brow. He lived only one glorious year and was my camping companion in the Adirondacks as well. He was born on a lake nearby and was fearless, as he would swim with me at Sandy Pond. He is buried down at the cabin.

"Cody"

Cody was my third Golden Retriever and spent all of his marvelous 15 years in and around the farm. He was named after Cody, Wyoming where Liz and I had recently visited. He and I explored all the hills and dales for miles together. He is buried down at the cabin.

"Max"

Max was Louise's first rescue Bichon and a true-blue member of the new blended family. Max could keep up with Cody and loved to explore all the hills and dales as well. He was fearless and faithful to the end. Max was 15 when buried down at the cabin.

"Archie"

Archie was a Wheaten Terrier who tried and failed to corral his two brothers, Max and Cody. Once Archie got lost in a wild rainstorm for hours and hours but eventually his instincts led him safely back to the farm, much to Louise's relief. He also had his moment in the sun herding a flock of George Gallagher's sheep who had escaped.

"Molly"

Molly was Louise's second rescue Bichon. She was an adorable, lovable, sweet dog. She loved the farm and her brothers. She was loyal and would always guard the domain for us. Her favorite time was luxuriating with Louise while the men went to the cabin! Molly may be buried at the cabin.

"Donnie"

Mike's Bichon "Donnie" has been a frequent guest at the farm. Donnie loves the freedom of the farmland and loves to explore. (See "Donnie Meets Bambi.") Donnie's signature move can come any time (in the middle of the

night) should an Owl hoot; he will run to the Castle
Tower with a howl of alarm!

"Bailey and Carli"

Two sister Bichons acquired in Florida after we lost
"Molly." Wonderful sisters!

About the Author

HENRY CARYL HALLAS is retired from various financial management positions in large corporations. He is a graduate of Yale University with a degree in history. Since the 1940's, he has spent extensive time living and vacationing in southern New Hampshire and has written a number of books solely for family and friends. This is his first effort to expand the audience.

OTHER BOOKS OF INTEREST

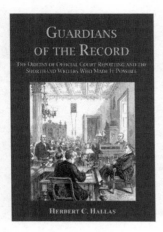

Guardians of the Record spotlights a group of remarkably interesting pioneer shorthand writers who were responsible for originating official court reporting in the United States. Many of them were reformers, some were entrepreneurs, and others were inventors, writers, artists, and scientists. All of them were skilled shorthand professionals. 221 pages. 70 illustrations. ISBN: 978-0-9977233-2-8.

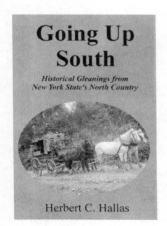

Going Up South is a collection of stories from New York State's North Country in the 19th century. It features: anti-Civil War activists; an outdoors-loving vice president; a radical preacher and feminist; Mohawk Indian lacrosse players; a widely-respected philosopher; a prominent U.S. Senator; a blind piano virtuoso; and sundry words of wisdom. 166 pages. 50 illustrations. ISBN: 978-0-9977233-0-4.

Made in the USA
Lexington, KY
06 September 2017